30 is a Dirty Word

by

Nishi Gulati

30 is a Dirty Word ©2025 by Nishi Gulati

ISBN: 979-8-218-92612-0

Dedication

To my parents, the unknowingly, naturally comedic geniuses, without whom this book would not be possible. Their love, support, and pursuit of my happiness are the pillars upon which this book rests. No words are enough to describe the meaningfulness of that foundation. Love you.

Acknowledgments

Writing this was harder, but more rewarding than I imagined. Many years in the making, this labor of love could not have been possible without some very important people:

My editor, Tanya Besmehn, whose positive vision saw this for all it could be and more; insightful guidance which helped make the characters and stories come alive; and knowledge, time, energy, and efforts that helped shape this entire book and make it finally come to be. Thank you for all you have done and continue to do.

My cousin Gaurav Sood, who thoughtfully and generously gave countless hours of his time helping me be directed and productive, reading, discussing, rereading, and honing each word of this book to allow me to see and reach my potential. I am sincerely appreciative.

My brother, Vineet Gulati, who honestly, thoughtfully, sometimes bluntly provided endless support and motivation to include moments almost forgotten, hone and sharpen the ironic humor, and most importantly keep going and do more than I imagined over the years to turn this idea from long ago into actually being. Thank you.

John B. Wren, a writer himself, who encouraged me to keep writing, publish, and to that end introduced me to Tanya Besmehn, who was key in making this book happen.

Mayank Austen Soofi, who with Gaurav, unselfishly provided insightful feedback to help develop and make the book its best version.

My close great friends and sister-in-law who all read various stages of this book and provided encouragement, positive feedback, and motivation to keep writing and dream big. I thank you all.

Last but certainly not least, my parents, Usha and Gene Gulati, who not only unwittingly provided the material, but whose limitless love, encouragement and support, have not only made this book possible, but also so much that is me.

Warning

It's often said that there are only two things certain in life—death and taxes. But I beg to differ. There is one other certainty, which can be equally painful and life-altering. Just ask those who have experienced it! What is this third *certainty* I speak of? If I have to spell it out, it means that you have yet to experience it. Be forewarned though, if you're a child, particularly a daughter, of Indian parents—it's coming. I don't want to sound melodramatic but calling it a *certainty* may be putting it mildly. A commandment from a higher power is more akin to the truth. Sounds laughable, I know. Trust me.

The truth is, if you live in my universe, when it comes to this matter, there is no laughter, not even a glimmer of a smile. As you all know, ridiculing a commandment would be blasphemy—blasphemy with consequences. Except, the consequences are not wrath or condemnation. However, if you've ever experienced the eternal guilt evoked by the tirades of a disappointed mother, you'll likely agree that the suffering is similar—if not worse.

Let me take a step back before talk of this "universe" begins to sound like science fiction, and tell you my story. The truth is, it actually exists. In this galaxy's black hole, I forget that not all universes are vortexes like mine.

I guess I should start at the beginning. Not the day I was born. Rather, when my second, and apparently, more important, life began.

CONTENTS

Boys
Friends or Foes?

B oys, friends or foes? It seems like a simple question. Yet, therapists have likely made millions discussing this very subject with Indian girls. And like many other issues for which that therapy couch stays occupied, this, too, must be the fault of our mothers.

Senior prom, the pre-eighteen wedding equivalent. Being the first such formal event for many of us meant it required planning and much thought about all the details. Most of us girls relished these major decisions: what we'd wear, how we'd have our hair done, who we'd ride with in the limousine, but, most importantly, who we'd go with. It was all part of the joy that marked the end of senior year, and my girls and I loved it.

Divya, Kayva, Veena, and I had been collectively laughing, crying, and discussing all of life's details, which were, of course, at presidential debriefing levels of importance, for the past decade. It had all started while jump-roping in recess during elementary school in our suburban New Jersey town, when a math workbook fell out of my half-zipped bookbag. I sheepishly started to pick it up and stuff it back into my bag when Veena approached me and said, "I have the same one. Do your parents make you do extra homework every weekend too?" I nodded, as both Divya and Kavya, who were turning the rope, chimed in, "Me too!"

Bonding over this cemented our friendship, and we became inseparable. So, when it came to prom, naturally, we did everything together. We spent hours in department store fitting rooms, buried to our waists in a sea of tulle and satin to find the perfect dress for each of us. Divya wanted a short dress, not because she thought it would be sexier, but because it would be more practical, which was her at the core. She was organized, determined, and the planner of our group. This allowed Kavya to be the dreamer and leader of "all that is fun!" And she didn't disappoint. Kavya was the vivacious one, throwing out exciting ideas, like, "Let's see Jerry Maguire in the theater!"

This set Divya in motion; she'd find the most practical movie times, gather adult reviews as to the appropriateness of the film for a quad of high school girls, and finally, present it all so politely to our parents, giving them little room to say "no." Together, they were the reason we saw Tom Cruise in all his glory on the big screen, got selfies with Veena's favorite Bollywood actor, Shah Rukh Khan, and danced the night away in our pajamas many Saturdays.

Divya's dress choice made sense—no extra material dragging on the ground to get stepped on. Plus, she justified her practicality by insisting it was easier to dance in something lightweight. She was picky, though, and didn't want something too tight, or too puffy either. Luckily, she wanted her dress in black; otherwise, Kavya would not have appreciated the competition for her grand entrance in the hot pink sequined mini dress with sky-high strappy heels she chose that should have been visible from space. She was all about the drama.

Veena wanted a traditional long ball gown dress that she thought signified prom, suiting her conservative personality. Veena was a hard worker and our resident brainiac, who hated being "shown up" at anything school related. She was a master at comparing grades, usually emerging the victor, complete with a glib remark of "better luck next time, girls." We were never offended; rather, it motivated us to try harder and top her.

I had wanted a classy long gown in a bright but understated color that put the 'e' in elegance. A mixture of traditional yet bold, standing out yet fitting in—that was the hardest to find, being the Hope Diamond of dresses. After what felt like the hundredth store we visited, I found my match. It was a gorgeous baby blue gown with pearl detailing and diamond cut-outs along the back, fit for the runway in my mind. Once we accomplished the monumental task of saying yes to the dress, we bought makeup so that Kavya's older sister could transform us into the Cinderellas of the hour, hoping the thickly applied mascara that none of us were used to wearing stayed put until the stroke of twelve. Our makeup had to complement not only our dresses but the first-ever manicures the four of us got. We all chose French manicures except Kayva, who opted for nails as bright as her dress.

Our endless trips to the mall, visits to the salon, and discussions ad nauseam of every detail may have made our parents rethink their decision to allow us to go to prom, but the four of us relished this celebrity-esque, glamorous occasion. I especially enjoyed all this because, like the well-trained child I was, I had done some advanced planning—almost four years' worth! I had focused my attention and energies on the most important part—*going with a date for the very first time!*

Now, before you jump the gun and start thinking that I was super organized and had sorted out who I'd go with, let me stop you. Why? Because before I got anywhere near the *who*, I needed to jump over the first, and most daunting hurdle—just going with a guy at all. Don't get me wrong, my problem wasn't a shortage of eligible guys. Although possibly skewed by her rose-colored glasses of best-friendship, Kayva was quick to point out all the guys she seemed to think were into me, apparently drawn to my approachable, friendly demeanor (I was always comfortable talking to anyone and a classic ENFJ—Extraverted, iNtuitive, Feeling, and Judging on the Myers-Briggs Type Indicator), plus what she termed my 100-watt smile. Rather, my dilemma lay in convincing my mother to let me leave the house on the arm of one. You see, Mom's ideas were based on the cultural norms of the society in which she was raised, which had fairly strict notions of propriety for girls, and although she no longer lived in India, she abided by those norms, because if not, *what would people say?* If they said anything at all, well then, what reputation of mine, and by extension, my family's would remain? You can take Indian parents out of India, but you can't take the *what would people say* out of them.

Societies evolve—couldn't my mom? Based on appearance, with her round face, soft features, and wide smile that exuded her naturally warm, friendly, and positive demeanor, everyone would say "why not?" It was true, Mom wasn't ultra-conservative. She wasn't against dressing up, dancing, or having fun with friends. In fact, she enjoyed all those things, thankfully for me. She even let me throw a huge pre-prom party at our house where almost half of the senior class came (I have always been into celebrating every occasion—life is too short not to). Granted, her motives weren't entirely borne of coolness.

If the get-together was at our place, she would know what was going on. She also didn't mind my going out with my girls—not without a curfew, of course. She had vetted them over the years, and they were similar to me, so she worried less. I say *less* rather than *not at all* because I'm not sure it's possible for moms, particularly mine, to not worry about their children. In truth though, there was nothing to really watch over since doing anything she and Dad disapproved of never really crossed my mind. But it wasn't me that she didn't trust; it was "the others." So, going to prom wasn't a problem. However, the thought of my going with someone of the opposite sex—well, obviously, that was out of the question, as "such an outlandish notion could only lead to no good." Besides, according to her, there was no need to go to prom with a boy when I could go with my friends and have just as much fun. Sure, going with Divya, Kavya, and Veena would have been nice. I was lucky to have such good friends to whom I could relate. Living in New Jersey meant that finding people similar to me was as ubiquitous as seeing a Starbucks on a New York City block. Our parents, all having come from India and raising their first-generation American children as a blend of two cultures meant that they generally valued the same things—education, education, education—and had similar ideas of acceptability. However, unlike our parents who wanted us to settle for a 'just fine' prom with friends, we girls wanted great, and that included going to prom with a date of the opposite sex. Given that it was going to be a tall mountain to climb, I had to start early, *very* early, if I had any hope of convincing Mom.

So, it began—a brief four-year (yes, you read correctly) conversation, aka relentless discussions, aka arguments, intermixed with begging and pleading, of course, to allow me to go to the senior prom with a boy. Now, I know you might be thinking, I could have just gone to the prom with a date without telling her, but again, defiance was not my style. Following the rules was just my way. So, it's a good thing that I'm very determined because I somehow won this battle. It may have taken years, but Mom actually let me go to prom with *a guy!*

Granted, there was nothing romantic between my prom date and I. Rohan, a school friend (obviously, Mom did not let me hang out with him outside of school), with whom I compared notes after tests, trying to guess how well we each had done, had asked me to prom first. Rohan and I, although both striving to get 'A's and taking the most challenging classes possible, weren't competitive with each other, or others for that matter, so we didn't mind being honest and enjoyed chatting with one another. We just weren't attracted to each other. He wasn't Brad Pitt, and I wasn't Cindy Crawford. Oh, and I was taller than him. These were the important things that mattered back then. But hey, a win was a win, and I'd take it. I use the term won loosely as winning should imply that the losing party learns something and changes their ways following defeat. However, wise adversaries such as Mom give their opponent a false sense of prolonged victory—then, they quietly strike again.

It is said that it takes ninety days to create a habit. That is, if one is interested in change. Apparently, neither Mom nor I were interested. Both of us were content with *my* ways. Socially, hanging out with my girls at one of our houses—mine being Mom's preferred go-to—going to dinner at Olive Garden (yes, that was the hot spot back then), doing dances for cultural events, playing basketball with my brother Ayaan and neighbors, or window-shopping at the mall were all I needed to have fun, and

Mom and Dad were good with all this. Well, that and my frequent phone conversations with friends in which we discussed the details of the day. This did get me in trouble with Mom and Dad at times, "All you do is talk, talk, talk. *Padhai pe dhyan laga liya karo*" as I should have been focusing on studying more according to them. Besides, "What will Ayaan learn watching you waste all your time on such silliness? What kind of example is 'Did you hear what xyz did?' He may start to think that 'As come from remembering what someone said rather than the Pythagorean theorem. 'XYZ' is for algebraic equations only. Don't lead him astray." Mom and Dad worried.

Ayaan was smart, naturally smarter than me for sure, but not exactly the hardest worker when it came to school. He didn't seem to worry about his future. Much to my parents' dismay, when he was a child, he aspired to be a garbage collector since they drove a "cool" truck. When later he heard that they made pretty good money, he thought it was the perfect job. He was always content. He was happy playing basketball, listening to music, and watching sports. The irony was that his natural abilities were such that he could be extremely successful. He was really good at math and architectural drawing. Mom knew it and spent hundreds of dollars enrolling him in all kinds of extracurricular educational activities to hopefully steer him in the only direction she could see—STEM.

I on the other hand worked hard and cared about doing well in school, so they didn't say too much. Besides, they were using a lot of their energy to get Ayaan to reach his potential. Overall, Mom and Dad were happy because I followed the rules, studied, and most importantly embodied their values like caring about people and doing the "right" thing. Occasionally, when I'd consider straying from their way of thinking, like wearing makeup when many of the girls in my class began to experiment with it, my parents would find a way to reel me in, "You don't need makeup to be beautiful, you already are." Or "It will hide your natural beauty." Flattery was their wise weapon of choice. Besides, I wasn't the experimental type by nature or nurture, so, as we all knew, I wasn't going to just do it. What was expected of "good" Indian children came naturally to me. Maybe this was another DNA engineering feat. That or the answering of the collective numerous, lengthy prayers of our parents.

Being my obedient, naive self unsurprisingly carried on from high school to college. Most people would probably label me as tame if they were to put it kindly. College is supposed to be about taking risks and making decisions independently. Given how deeply my parents had etched my brain with their compendium of notions of proper behavior for a single young girl, our relationship, and my nature, I, for the most part, thought it best to talk to Mom and Dad before engaging in and making most life choices. *Whose life was it again?*

Yes, I was out of state at college and had the freedom that distance afforded me, but I still went to them before making large decisions. Forget out of state, I did that even when an ocean stood between us as I studied abroad in London during the first semester of my second year. One Friday night after returning from yet another dinner where I was offered wine, I decided to call home for answers. I put on my soft cotton pajamas and curled up on the bed of my dorm room trying to get comfortable for an uncomfortable conversation, as I dialed our home number on the landline.

Mom picked up the phone, "*Beta,*" the Hindi word for *child* that Mom and Dad use to lovingly address Ayaan and I, "*kaise ho?*" asking how I was doing. I pictured them parked on our comfy family room sofa, watching their favorite Hindi soap opera in which the show's background music blared as the camera panned across all the characters' faces reacting to the latest almost shocker. I eased into my reason for calling. "I went to dinner with one of my advisors, his wife, and a few other students…" Mom was thrilled that I was socializing and rubbing shoulders with other intellectuals. "The food was good," I went on, "but here the drinking age is eighteen, and they serve wine with meals." I felt my face scrunch as I said the next words, "What do you and Dad think about me trying it?" The initial silence was deafening, "Mom? Are you there?" I could picture her face, brow furrowed, sudden stress marring her generally smooth complexion.

"Drinking! At this age? Oh beta, what are you saying? You're way too young for all that! On top of that, you're alone in a foreign country. If something happens, we're not there. No, no, no!"

"But it's totally normal here, everyone drinks, and they are all fine. And I wouldn't be drinking much at all, just trying it."

"That may be the case, but you're a smaller person, so it will affect you more than others. Also, you've never had it, so you won't know how much is too much. Actually, most people don't realize when they've had too much. That's the effect of alcohol. If you must try it, we'll think about it later when you're at home, with Dad, and after you're twenty-one," she implored as Dad concurred. I wondered if she really meant that, or it was like a campaign promise.

What was a girl to do? Every time I went out, I was stuck between a rock and a hard place. I could either be the weird girl who didn't want to have fun. Or I could be the guilt-ridden girl who didn't listen to her parents who had crossed an ocean with nothing for her brighter future. Ignorance was definitely bliss. I would have been so much better off not asking, and assuming that legally okay was the line. Since neither option was great, I went with the best middle-ground plan I could think of—if offered a drink, I would accept and just hold the glass without really drinking it for a while and then set it down when no one was paying attention. This actually worked decently well, so I used it for the next few years. I'm conflict averse. Trust me, I know how laughable and *different* this all sounds, but what can I say, other than, that was just me.

The struggle bus continued onward to *dating lane*. During the second semester of my second and last year in college, I met an attractive guy in a premed (surprise, surprise, I was going to be a doctor) organic chemistry class, who asked me to grab brunch with him at the dining hall that weekend as we finished our latest experiment in one of our Thursday evening lab sessions. Chemistry in chemistry—miracles and science apparently can mix. Instead of just accepting his invitation to brunch like most, I headed back to my dorm room to call Mom and get her thoughts, knowing instinctively she'd reject the idea. Imagine my surprise when she simply said, "Yes. Go." *What???* My jaw was on the floor. *No multi-year battles?!* No calling out to the gods to save my soul, questioning where society had led me astray, or exhorting me to focus on the number one priority in life, education/career? No need for the input of Dad or other aunties? I didn't understand. I was at a complete loss. It appeared to my naive mind that my prom victory had created true change, and I felt glorious. Oh, so glorious. *Time to revel!*

Naivete is hard to break free from. I'd say my glory days were short-lived, but nonexistent would be more accurate. One night a few weeks later, Mom called as she did nightly for us to catch up. "What are you doing tonight?" she had asked. "Going to dinner with Raj," I absentmindedly replied as I pumped my natural, dark curls trying to get them to have volume but not frizz.

"What? Just the two of you? At this late hour (it was 6 pm)? What do you mean? You're not seriously thinking of going alone with him are you, Nikki? What will people say? Why do you need to go? What are you planning on doing? Why didn't either one of you invite anyone else? Why isn't your roommate coming along? Invite her. She's a lovely girl. In fact, let me speak with her and invite her for you. She likes me and will listen to me."

Clearly the word "date" had gotten lost in translation somehow. I mean, Mom had *only* lived in the US for over twenty years at that point, but what was two whole decades when it came to this matter? Oh sure, I was allowed to "date" in college, as long as I didn't actually go on any dates. Apparently, dates only involved groups of people, never just two—did I miss the memo on this? Oh wait, smartphones were not yet a thing, so clearly, I could not be blamed. I say that as if post smartphones with constant access and notifications up the wazoo, I suddenly became like the superstar employee reading and responding to all emails within the hour. Totally comical—I'm clearly into making jokes. Apparently, this dating business was never really approved.

My parents' dislike of dating, like many other Indian parents, was twofold. First, obviously, boys were no good. They had raging hormones that tempted nice girls into doing unacceptable things before marriage. By *unacceptable things,* I mean any displays of physical affection, such as the highly risky handholding. I've already spoken of enough impropriety, so I won't venture further to the incomprehensible. If I was engaged in such a jumping out of a plane without a parachute-type activity, how could I succeed? How could I, as a first-generation child in this country, accomplish the things Mom and Dad had immigrated here for me to achieve? How could I create a life free from the struggles and obstacles they faced when they came to this country with nothing but eight dollars in their pocket? Not with handholding, that's for sure. Actually, exactly with handholding, just the hands of my parents, not the tempting hands of boys. That's why God gave us two hands you know—one for each parent to tightly clasp in their death grip. If your hands are preoccupied, you can't touch anything else. Reach out and touch someone does not apply to Indian girls. It's important to read the fine print.

The second, and if not a more important reason behind my parents' dislike of dating was what people would say if they saw me with a boy! Indian parents love to "talk". On Saturday afternoons, Mom and her friends would get together for their "kitty parties". They would sit around in the family room, drink cups of steaming hot chai and snack on freshly prepared samosas and other snacks while chatting up a storm. Children were not invited, but when these parties were at our house, I'd inadvertently overhear what they'd talk about.

"How is your son, Seema? Did he get his SAT results? He must have. Did he too get a sixteen hundred like my Raja? It's okay if he didn't. It's very rare to get a perfect score, you know, and not everyone can be accepted to Harvard," one aunty said to another, who awkwardly straightened her Kurti top, looked down at her teacup and quickly rushed to refill her barely drunk chai.

"My Neil is always volunteering and helping people. Did you all see his picture in the local paper receiving his community service award?" another aunty proudly asked the group as she stood up to better see the "should be" impressed faces.

If the conversation happened to revolve around you, it was often embarrassing. Praise was as difficult to accept as disappointment; one had you blushing, the other had you fighting back tears. Would we children ever be "good enough"? I often made a note of what *not* to do to my own children one day.

Whether it was my cousin Akshay repeatedly making the honor roll, or Veena's sister Jaya's perfect attendance, the bragging rights ran rampant—until they morphed into gossip.

"Do you know what I saw while shopping yesterday? The aunty paused for dramatic effect while the others realized the boasting fest had ended. "Neena's daughter standing next to some boy! She was smiling and looking at him. I saw him laugh and touch her hand! This too in the neighborhood during the daytime!" this aunty exclaimed to the group while placing her hand on her heart and dropping her jaw in horror.

"Definitely something is going on between them. What is happening these days? I tell you, these girls are given way too much freedom. They're becoming American. Next thing you know, they too will be wearing those tiny skirts," another aunty added, shaking her head in despair.

"My Sheila would never do such a thing. We've given our daughters the proper values," the first aunty said while looking up to the heavens to quietly thank God. The others followed, equally grateful that God had spared their daughters from such calamity.

From all this, one would surmise that boys were clearly foes from which distance, preferably with a five-foot radius, must be kept at all times. "Safety first," they always say. They also say, "When you assume, you make an ass of yourself." *Dang*, why are *they* always right?

The obedient child I was, I followed the unspoken but nonetheless enforced mantra "stay away from boys" as best as I could. Other than the one guy I "dated" in college, there was no one else I was romantically involved with during the next few years. I was convinced by Mom and Dad that I had to have a singular focus to succeed. Since it had worked at allowing me to graduate college in two years and getting me into and through medical school, there seemed to be no reason to abandon the path. Besides, to be honest, I was content within my bubble of family and friends. As you are by now aware, I was naive, with simple pleasures, and an old soul. I was genuinely happy. It was a few months to medical school graduation, and I had already matched into a residency for the specialty of my choice. My hard work had paid off, and my life for the next few years was planned. The natural trajectory of medicine, where the next steps are planned well in advance, suited my personality. That meant it was finally time to relax, be proud of what I had accomplished thus far, and do the things I would have little time for during the next four years. Or so I thought. Apparently, I had not yet done enough. One successful career in medicine was simply just slacking off.

"Beta, now that your career is set, it's high time for you to meet someone. Is there anyone you know? Anyone in your medical school? There must be many nice eligible boys. Any of them you're interested in?" Mom asked during one of our daily catch-up calls where much of the conversation centered around my diet and if I had indeed consumed all the lentils and veggies she had made and sent with me from my last visit home.

I was dumbfounded into silence, which, if you know me, happens as rarely as a solar eclipse. Before my brain could reach left field, where Mom's thoughts seemed to be coming from, she chimed in again, "You can tell us you know? Dad and I are your friends. You can tell us anything. If there is someone, you let us know so that we can meet him and talk to his parents about moving things forward," Mom then continued on about the openness of the parent-child relationship. Enough said.

"I'm giving the phone to Dad. He wants to talk to you." I could hear Mom in the background calling for Dad to pick up the phone and explain "it" to me. I'm sure she figured that Dad, who was naturally calm, easygoing, and better with words, would have greater success with this conversation. Dad, with his white hair, glasses, and comfortable evening and weekend athleisure wear, slowly walked over to take the phone. Now this was going to be an awkward conversation. Dad, although being born and raised in India, was in many ways, like us first generation children—neither here nor there—a mix of traditional yet not conservative. Dad, like many traditional men, focused on working and earning money, and for the most part, left Mom in charge of the rest. So, if we wanted to talk about or get permission for something, we went to Mom. Also, she was the more lenient of the two. Yet, he was the one who reviewed our homework and helped us study for tests when we were younger. Like many men of his generation, Dad was the silent, practical, unemotional type who didn't get involved in things like gossip. He was the world news-watching, serious type. Yet he often cracked "dad jokes," which he of course thought were hilarious.

He was traditional like Mom in certain ways, like wanting me to learn how to cook, but surprisingly not so in wanting Ayaan to learn as well. He wanted both Ayaan and I to learn to do everything for ourselves. Dad practiced what he preached. He made all the typical foods we regularly ate, including rotis (the round flatbreads) so well, he put some aunties to shame. Growing up, both Ayaan and I had the same curfew. The only difference was that Ayaan broke curfew often, and got away with it, while that never flew for me. I often asked Ayaan how he managed to get such liberties, but we both knew that nothing would properly explain that that was just how it was for boys and girls in an Indian household.

"Hi Nikki beta, Mom and I were talking, and we were thinking, you need to start meeting people. This is the perfect time and age. You no longer have the same pressures of school like you did the last few years, so you can meet boys and find a suitable partner. Anyone you have in mind?"

"Dad, what's the rush? Seriously, where's the fire? Why do I need to meet someone all of a sudden? Why can't I just see what happens in life?" I asked.

"Who said anything about rushing? Everything should just be in the proper time. All we're saying is that the time to meet prospective boys is now. If you don't start meeting boys at this time, then how will you get married?"

Wait, what? Married? Who were these two? My parents weren't spontaneous people. They were predictable, eat the same oatmeal for breakfast, have the same hair style, follow the exact routine for years, kind of people. Mom couldn't keep a secret and therefore didn't know how to throw surprise parties or keep gifts for any occasion hidden. She wasn't one to make jokes either. Neither truly understood or knew what sarcasm was, and they certainly didn't throw curveballs like this. Seemed like just a minute ago we were sitting outside the pool and now we were doing cannonballs into the deep end. Zero to sixty in less than a second? This from the two people who drove below the speed limit in the middle lane and thought that was fast!

"Get married? Dad, I'm only twenty-two. I have all the time in the world to think about that. Right now, I want to enjoy the fact that I don't have to worry about taking any more exams and just chill with my friends before everyone moves away for residency. What you're saying is crazy." I couldn't hide my exasperation.

"We're not saying you have to get married tomorrow, but if you don't start looking now, then how will it be possible?"

"Dad, there is so much time, years in fact! And why do I even have to look? The right person will come along at some point, which isn't now!"

"Beta, if you don't look, then how will you find the right person? You haven't been looking and haven't met anyone yet, so taking an active approach is necessary," Dad said as if stating the most obvious, simplistic fact.

"Dad is right. You haven't found a boy up 'till this point. You won't meet anyone just sitting at home and

17

waiting. No one is going to fall into your lap," Mom chimed in matter-of-factly. That statement was coming from Mom, who met Dad when he came to see her at her house after hearing from acquaintances that my mom was single and to be arranged into marriage!

I was shocked and confused. Yet, I could do nothing but laugh at the irony of it all.

I realized then that I had been trying to solve a mystery that didn't even exist. "Boys, friends or foes" had appeared to me to be an *a* or *b* multiple choice question whose answer was based on gathered evidence. Naivete once again, looking for depth in a mirage of water. I had overlooked the literality of it all. It was self-evident, staring me in the face the entire time. The *or* didn't imply a choice but instead was a fact. It wasn't a question at all, but rather a statement! Boys were foes or "friends" (aka spouses), just like on or off switches.

I should have known. Isn't that how humans work? Well, at least Indian girls, since our IT and engineering parents had programmed us that way.

Time to Wear Red Proactively

The decree had been issued. I was to meet someone. Now, you might think that that implied allowing the natural course of events to unfold. I'd go about my daily life, and along the way, meet a smart, witty, handsome, successful, genuinely nice guy. We'd date, he'd turn out to be the one, and we'd eventually get married. Sounds straight-forward enough, right? Not to Mom and Dad, who saw nothing but glaring red flags in the above, being subject to the vagaries of life and time. Mom and Dad didn't like to leave things to chance, as that did not align with the Hinduism concept of karma, which essentially means action. Hindus believe that we have control over our actions, but not the outcome. My parents are devout believers, so action they took.

One morning when I was at home, me and the family, minus Mom, who was standing at the stove as usual, were sitting around the glass kitchen table in our usual spots (guys on one side, girls on the other) having breakfast and chatting. "How'd you do on that paper Mom *made* me help you on? I'm sure you got an A since I practically wrote it!" I smugly asked Ayaan, who was lazily lounging in his chair, his feet propped on the chair next to mine.

"I did, but that's because of the finishing touches I put on it," said Ayaan, jokingly as he pushed up his eyeglasses. He may have been younger than me, but he thought he was older and wiser. It didn't help that other people often thought he was older because of his signature short beard, glasses, and stature. He wasn't a really big guy, but I was a fairly petite girl, and he was taller than me by at least half a foot.

"And you claim I'm the favorite. Mom has never had you *help* me with any of my work. And look, she made aloo parathas just for you," I said pointing to the growing stack of freshly made potato stuffed flatbreads as mom flipped another paratha on the tawa, or circular griddle.

"Oh, you're definitely the favorite. And don't worry, Mom's making your favorite cauliflower parathas too. Shouldn't you be helping her over there? I'm sure your future husband will appreciate you making him fresh parathas," said Ayaan sarcastically, laughing hysterically. I rolled my eyes and swatted towards his arm but caught the edge of his sweatshirt. The Anand men had been sporting athleisure well before it became the universal cool wear.

"Guys, shouldn't Nikki be learning how to make parathas for her future husband?" Ayaan asked, turning towards Mom and Dad, changing his facial expression to a mockingly serious one.

"Ayaan, yes, Nikki should be learning, but so should you, beta. You know I believe that it's important for everyone, both girls and boys, to know how to cook," said Dad in his even-tempered tone. His diplomacy was actually genuine. "Ayaan does bring up an important subject though. Speaking of a future husband for you, Nikki beta, we need to be proactive in this matter. We must take charge. Mom and I think you must join this Indian matrimonial website," said Dad matter-of-factly, suddenly turning our light discussion into one I wasn't prepared for.

"You know Ami aunty and her eldest daughter Puja, right? And you know they were looking for someone for Puja, right? Well, Ami told me that this site is how Puja met her fiancé! The boy is from the same town as them, and lives nearby, only a few streets away. They're getting married at the end of this year, and Ami tells me they are all very happy," Mom announced, brimming with excitement. What could possibly be better than secondhand success stories from Mom's friends? This matrimonial website's credibility had just been proven beyond a shadow of a doubt. Attempting to bolster her point, Mom added, "You must talk to Ami aunty's daughter yourself. She'll tell you. I'll call Ami today and get Puja's number for you." Just what I had needed, another uncomfortable conversation on a Saturday.

Now you might be thinking, *online dating, no big deal. Everyone's doing it.* Sure, it's the norm these days. Fifteen to twenty years ago, back in the early 2000s, though, it was like wearing a scarlet letter. It was something you only admitted to if caught in the act. It was the time when every guy you met would say, "If this works out, let's tell people we met at Starbucks or something." Besides, Indian parents and Puritans are pretty much interchangeable.

"This is crazy and totally unnecessary. I really don't know why we, or should I say you guys, are even considering this!" I looked to Ayaan for support, but he was taking far greater pleasure in seeing me squirm as he nodded in whole-hearted agreement with Mom and Dad. Of course he was. They weren't pressuring him to meet someone. In fact, Mom and Dad didn't even discuss dating or marriage with him because as they said, a single educated guy didn't need such help, as girls and or their parents would seek him out. More importantly, unlike me,

21

apparently, he had lots of time for this. Guys don't become "spinsters" after all.

"Beta, you're not being reasonable. You're not thinking ahead. Right now, you only meet people in your school. With this website, you'll meet *ladka* from all over. Plus, it's an Indian site, so those on it are looking for the same types of things as us. We also know someone it worked for, so rejecting it without even trying it doesn't make sense. And you haven't met anyone on your own, so this is the only way," said Dad.

There it was rearing its ugly head again, the fact that I had not met anyone, despite not actually being *allowed to meet anyone!* I was certain I was far too young for marriage. I was raised in the U.S. but trapped in the cultural confines of India. To them, those ideas were the only right ways. It was futile to argue, it was two against one, and I was definitely on the losing end of this argument.

When Mom and Dad decide something needs to be done, they don't waste time and take care of it right away. Dad loves to recite "What you can do tomorrow, do today. What you can do today, do now." It's unfortunate that that gene wasn't passed on. Ayaan and I are the opposite, procrastinators to a fault. Mom and Dad had become accustomed to our ability to avoid a request or chore until the last possible moment.

I guess twenty-two years was enough for Mom and Dad to wise up. So, they didn't even ask me to sign up for this website. Dad took it upon himself. Now, I know that he and Mom must have really wanted this because Dad is not technologically savvy. Like, not at all. Remembering how to copy and paste things on the computer was a major technological accomplishment for him. A feat worthy of praise, followed by a much-needed rest to recover from such exertion.

One gloomy winter weekend when it was so cold that even the sun didn't want to come out, both Mom and Dad seemed to be busy with their usual weekend routine. Mom was chopping cauliflower, fire-roasting eggplants that would later become *bharta*, and cooking *dhals* (lentil soups) for dinners that week. It was easier to meal-prep on a weekend since she worked full-time as an engineer. Dad was rifling through papers while simultaneously on his computer. Intermittently I could hear him clicking away on the laptop when I took stretch breaks from watching TV in bed. I made nothing of it, assuming he was doing something for work, as he was often reading and writing scientific research articles on the weekends. A couple of hours later, Dad called "Nikki beta, come down here and take a look at this. All we need to do now is to upload a photo and we're done!"

"Look at what, Dad?" I asked as I flipped channels during the commercials.

"What do you mean, '*what?*' Have you forgotten already? Mom and I talked to you about joining that matrimonial site. Now it's almost done. Just this last thing is remaining for which I'm calling you. Hurry up."

Oh God! They were actually serious! Ignorance really is bliss. Fear doesn't come close to describing the "disaster is imminent" feeling that had risen within me as I dragged myself downstairs to the family room where Dad was sitting on the couch. Cautiously squinting at the computer screen, I saw a profile that shockingly didn't make me want to throw up. It was relatively basic. Dad had answered the ridiculous required profile questions on the site as minimally as possible.

Luckily for him, most answers were self-evident. For body type, slim was appropriate. The oh, so flattering other choices of average, athletic, and heavy didn't at all apply to me. For skin complexion, again luckily for him, one of the only two answers deemed desirable for women according to most Indian people of my parent's generation and prior, very fair and fair, matched me. Dad hadn't answered the optional, but clearly very important, questions such as blood type. Even in the section of the profile reserved for self-description, Dad had included my basic academic details and a few descriptive adjectives. Those descriptors, beautiful, fair, slim, family-oriented, good balance between eastern and western culture, were standard verbiage for parents of "the girl." No added fluff. None. This was more than sufficient. In fact, it was comprehensive according to Dad. Would it have been my way of describing myself? *Do I even have to answer that?* But it wasn't untrue and was a million times better than what I had feared.

The best part was that at the top of the page, it clearly stated who had posted the profile—another requirement of the site. I was off the hook of shame—well, at least as much as I could have been. I could wear my scarlet red on the inside for now.

"Anything else you would like to add?" Dad asked. It included my height, body type, complexion color, lack of prior marital status, education, and "mother tongue." Oh, and a list of interests like tennis, aerobics (our people's equivalent of working out I suppose), cooking, reading, etc. that one could check off. What more could a girl want to say about herself? If this wasn't the best promotion of me, what would be?

"If not, then let us look for a good photo of you. Show me which ones you have." Oh lord, it was getting worse.

I had thought about claiming that I didn't have any pictures, which wouldn't have been too much of a stretch. I never remembered a camera when going out. Yes, at that time, cell phone cameras weren't a thing. Like at all. I barely had any pictures from the last few years. In fact, I had to borrow pictures from a friend for my section of our medical school yearbook. Before I could decide how to feign a complete lack of vanity and thus having no pictures, Dad remembered having seen some in an album in my room.

Very hesitantly, I pulled out the few pictures that I had. Dad started going through the limited options and seemed to like one a bit more than the others. This sparked Mom's interest, and she walked over to get a first-hand look. "Are these all the pictures you have? Don't you have any better ones? What are you wearing in this one?" Before I could say anything, she turned to Dad, "This is the one you selected? This isn't good at all. Look at what's in the background! We need an appropriate picture that represents us." The picture was taken in front of a famous sculpture at the Louvre. It was nude. It was by DaVinci. It was classic awe-worthy art to be studied and displayed in the finest museums. Well, according to everyone but Indian parents.

Fortunately for society, we are math and science people. Had we been artists, brightly colored clothing would have covered every masterpiece. In fact, we do it now. Mom, like they do in temples, dresses the idols of our Gods in carefully chosen outfits. And God cannot just have one outfit. The outfits must change for the various religious occasions. I mean, to be seen in the same outfit more than once? Blasphemy. And it's not at all just my mom. There is a whole industry for this, hence the ability to go clothes shopping for religious idols. "Clothes are what make the body look beautiful. Otherwise, it's not good-looking," Mom would say. And I stand corrected, the sculptures and art were *awe-worthy* to Indian parents, just more like "awe no, how can such obscenity be displayed publicly. Cover it up, and don't stand near such things. You shouldn't be associated with the likes of such. What will people say?"

I had thought it was a nice picture of me. Apparently, that didn't matter. Clearly, I had no perspective, and my priorities were warped. I had thought that the background was less important than the subject. Untrue. I had also thought the background conveyed my love of traveling and appreciation of art. Wrong again. Maybe if the sculpture was wearing a red wedding sari, it would have been different. Dad then thought about the target audience and reconsidered, hoping to avoid any possible negative reaction emails from potential suitors' parents. If my own mother had such a strong reaction to the picture, what would other parents say? Are you starting to see how it always comes back to that? Oh, and you heard correctly, I said potential suitors. Yes, this is a fairytale produced by an animation powerhouse.

Mom and Dad continued to sift through the photos, finding some flaw in each, and in turn, slowly sucking the self-esteem out of me. My outfits were drab, or worse, too revealing, my hair was too curly, too straight, too unruly, I was too thin, too casual, too plain—I wished that I could melt into the couch cushion and disappear like yesterday's Dorito crumbs.

"That shirt neck needs another button. Did it break? It must have! Give that shirt to me and I will fix it. Until then, I don't want you wearing that shirt. What will people think?" Mom exclaimed, visibly frustrated.

"Look at her arms in this sleeveless top," Dad said with a firm shake of his head, "that won't do. She looks too skinny."

"Ahh, you're right. Boys don't like that," agreed Mom.

"Find one where she's wearing loose clothing. She'll look a little plumper and boys would prefer that," suggested Dad.

"No, in those she'll appear swallowed by the clothes, and besides, boys prefer flattering clothing," disagreed Mom.

They finally settled on one—not because they liked it—but it was the one they disagreed on the least. Marriage is about compromise after all. Once that monumental task was accomplished, Dad finalized the process by paying for a six-month subscription. It was a better deal than the one-month subscription after all. Practical and fiscally responsible—could it be any more ideal?

With that, it was done. I was officially online. *Let mating season begin.*

Turns Out...

Online dating is the norm today. Yes, some people still feel there's a stigma associated with meeting the love of their life on a 2-inch LED screen. But it's no longer a jaw-dropper to hear that's how a relationship that ended up with 12 bridesmaids and a reception hall dance floor of 350 partying guests got started. Twenty years ago, though, that was not at all true. Online dating was relatively new and filled with questions and concerns. While it would seem that those questions and concerns would be the same for an Indian dating website as for any other, that too was false. Why? The myriad of reasons deserves a deep dive—too bad not to see the brightly colored Great Barrier Reef floor, but more like into the bizarre Wonderland awaiting after tumbling down this long rabbit hole.

Being on an Indian matrimonial website was not quite what you might think. Maybe some of you are thinking that it would have been enjoyable and exciting, bringing with it the possibility of meeting one's soulmate. That's a very romantic thought, and I applaud your positivity, but you would be naïve like me, and unfortunately wrong. You see, that's idealistic and all sunshine and rainbows. Over here, we're talking reality. Sure, an altered version of reality, but the reality of many of us first generation Indian girls, nonetheless, and let me tell you, there was nothing romantic about this.

Indian matrimonial sites had one big difference from other online dating platforms (aside from the obvious: no one was joining these sites to hook up)—one was a family affair, and one was personal. Can you guess which was which? How was that even possible, you ask? You see, on these Indian sites, a profile could be created by anyone for anyone. It wasn't required that the person whose profile it was put it up themselves. The norm on these sites was that parents created the profiles. This seed, from which all the weeds of issues stemmed, was like one of Jack's deceptive magic beans. *Turns out*, Indian dating websites were *not* actually dating sites at all. While they may have had the new age online element, Indian matrimonial sites were just updated versions of good old arranged marriage.

Now before you tell me that I should have known better, let me say it for you. Turns out, it was my usual naivete and thus missing the obvious. I mean, the website name had the wording wedding in it. Plus, there was the long-standing history regarding "dating" that should have tipped me off. "What is this dating?" Mom and Dad would ask. "There is married and not married. And if you're dating, then you're not married. If you're not married, then you're wasting time."

I tried long and hard over the years to explain the idea of dating as the way to getting to know someone, but it was largely lost on Mom and Dad. Honestly, I'm not sure what I was expecting anyway. Another of Dad's favorite Hindi sayings loosely translates into "quick engagement, and even quicker wedding." *I know, what father of a girl say that?* Mine, that's who. But it's not at all related to rushing to the altar to avoid a baby bump, dispelling the mirage of the white wedding dress as you may be thinking. Hear my parents' story and you'll understand. That, or you'll be twice as surprised.

Both my parents are from a country and a generation in which the common way to get married was through an arranged marriage. I'm not saying that there weren't couples who got married after falling in love, but given that those unions were named "love marriages," you can understand just how rare they were. More than rare, they were taboo.

The way in which it worked was simple. Parents started by asking everyone they knew if there was a suitable boy for their daughter amongst their family, friends, and acquaintances. If that sure-fire method did not generate enough leads, parents placed a matrimonial advertisement in the newspaper to find suitors. Reading in the paper that "Parents of x background and religion were searching for a smart, educated, professional boy of the same background for their fair, tall, homely, and university graduate girl" was the norm. This garnered responses from the families of eligible men, which would typically include contact information and a request to receive a photograph of the girl. If the stars aligned, the boy's family would arrange a convenient mutual time with the girl's family for an initial meet and greet, not unlike today's version of buying a used car on Craigslist: you're intrigued by the photo, the low mileage, the fact that it's been garage-kept...you get the idea.

However, at times, the boy's family would arrive at the girl's house *unannounced* to get a "real look" at the girl and her family. The underlying premise of all visits was to judge the girl to see if she was *good enough* for the *prized* boy. Don't get me wrong, there was judgment and thus potential for rejection or approval on both sides, but these visits were the boy's family coming to see the girl.

A benign visit would typically include the boy's family speaking first with the girl's family, the girl then being asked to enter the room by bringing and serving tea and snacks to the prospective family, and then sitting down, eyes averted, answering any questions. The questions could range from the girl's education, interests, ability to cook, family-oriented-ness, etc. The girl's family could ask similar questions of the boy, although they were usually confined to work and education. If this wasn't enough, some guys' parents took it one step further and behaved as though they were going to an open market to buy livestock, measuring the girl, assessing her bloodline, seeing how her coat, sorry, hair and skin, shone, and judging her cooking to determine if it she would be a working or *show* wife.

If both families liked each other's child for their own, the relationship was cemented with a verbal agreement, sweets, and talk of speaking to the family priest regarding an auspicious day for the wedding. Now I'm not saying that all relationships started this way, but this was the norm in many cities at that time. Occasionally, the girl and boy were allowed to talk alone at that visit or even meet without a whole host of people once engaged, but that was far less common, and more for those who were "liberal" in their thinking.

One of Mom's favorite stories from when she was in college dealt with a boy who had asked her if she would go see a movie with him. Mom had replied, "You guys want a girl that has never been out with a boy, but yet you want to take me out now? Absolutely not. Don't even think of it." Even if she had ever thought of going, my grandfather would have forbidden it. *What would society say, after all?* I digress.

Getting back to how Mom and Dad met. My grandparents had been looking for a suitable match for some time for Mom. A steady stream of boys and their families had come and gone, but nothing had clicked. Then came my father. He had returned to India to visit his family after studying in the U.S. for a few years. He was on winter break from his graduate studies and was interested in finding a wife. He had seen Mom's matrimonial advertisement, corresponded with her parents, and arrived at their home with an elder brother soon after his return to India. My dad and uncle spoke with my maternal grandparents, Mom served them tea, they all talked for a short while, and the rest is history. Dad liked what he saw and told his family he wanted to marry her.

Their parents corresponded and a date was set; they'd marry in two weeks, becoming officially engaged the day before the ceremony as was customary. Yes, Mom and Dad had only met once at her home. Yes, they were going to be joined in holy matrimony for lifetimes—seven minimum according to Hindu traditions, but who knows how many exactly since as Hindus we believe in reincarnation. But why delay after all? Obviously, there could not be a single good reason. They've been happily married for 45 years, so what do I know? *Turns out,* less *is* more, and growth isn't always good. Sometimes, like algae, it muddies the waters.

All is Fair
in Love and War

Having a profile amounted to almost nothing in and of itself. What came from the process of monitoring the profile was what mattered. Now, given that it was my profile, it would seem logical that I would be the one checking it. However, I wasn't motivated or "serious" enough for Mom and Dad, so Dad made it his job to ensure that I was on the matrimonial train. Anything worthwhile requires hard work, after all, *they* say, and our people are good at hard work. We've been trained from a very young age. So, why wouldn't we be willing to jump over a few extra hurdles in this area as well? I mean, who doesn't enjoy and desire to put in the work of wading through a sea of profiles to go on endless first dates for something like meeting someone? Isn't that everyone's dream way to spend many weekends of some of the best years of life?

Every weekend, Dad would turn on the computer, login to the website and wade through the sea of responses that my profile had garnered. Remember, he was not technologically savvy. What is a simple man such as himself to do to keep track of all the activity? Obviously, write it all in a notebook. Dad got a wide-ruled spiral notebook, wrote *Nikki's God-Willing Prosperous Future* on the cover, and inked the date and details of the first boy who expressed interest in me. At that time, Dad was unaware of the copious amount of space that would be required for the astounding number of entries that would be painstakingly recorded over numerous years, so he foolishly wrote only one entry per page. Clearly, he had not learned of paper and tree conservation in India. Also, I now see where I get my naivete from.

Although Dad was doing all the website monitoring, he only saw himself as the medium between the potential boys and me. Any time I was home, Dad would open the website and have me sit next to him to complete my "homework" under his watch. Together we would go through each interest received. We would read the boy's profile and check out the accompanying pictures if there were any. Having a picture was not required on this website. If one did have a picture, the picture could be openly displayed or visible only to paying members. Then he would ask me if I was interested. If I was, he would find that boy's profile page in his notebook, write that I had agreed and said "yes", and then make a note for himself to send an email conveying my interest and requesting further information. This "interest" went from one parent to another as on both ends it was parents managing the profiles. This automatically made parents the go-betweens, which may seem tedious and undesirable for them, but was actually relished by many of them. Parents loved to be involved, and in many ways, controlling the gates that allowed access to the apples of their eyes.

Not to be cliche, but many boys' mothers especially loved the opportunity to exert some control over the choice of their future daughter-in-law. You could hear parents' sense of pride and accomplishment in having obedient children who *"appreciated"* their *"help"* and opinions when they spoke about it at gatherings. While their friends lapped it up and were impressed, me and the others being "shopped" knew better. Their children had essentially no choice, and silence does not equal appreciation.

Dad's notebook notations may seem like overkill to you, and definitely did to me, but to Dad, it was like an insurance policy. Sometime later, he would ask whether or not I had communicated with said boy, and if I hadn't, Dad would whip out his notebook, turn to the corresponding page, and point to the evidence. My agreement was there in ink for all to see. It was a trap that I continuously got caught in.

My saying "yes" was only the start of a journey akin to a trek through a desert in search of water. As "*dho hath say thali baj thi hai*," there needed to be another to do this tango. The journey could go a few different ways at that juncture, and most were not pretty.

Road one, worst-case scenario: the guy I was saying "yes" to had no clue who I was. What else could be expected with one of the worst problems with being on these sites, when it went from a family affair to a solely parental affair? What do I mean? Our parents were tough, and they didn't take "no" well. If their children didn't want to partake in this matrimonial process, they would do it for them. So, many guys had no idea they were being paraded on an Indian match-and-meet site. On top of that, oftentimes, guys were already embedded in a relationship unbeknownst to their parents because they, A: Wouldn't approve, or B: Doubly wouldn't approve. Either way, an attached person being touted as fair game on a dating website does not bode well for anyone. It's somewhat deceitful if we're calling a spade a spade. Unintentional deceit, so I guess it's not as bad as intentional deceit, which happened as well. In these situations, parents knew that their son or daughter was dating someone, but didn't like said significant other, so decided that putting them on a matrimonial site was the clear solution to their "attachment" problem.

"Dear parents of Nikki, we are writing to inquire as to whether Nikki has received an email from our son Prakash? We fear that he may be delaying due to this Gujarati girl in his medical school who took a liking to him before he graduated. She seems to be after him, but we're sure our Prakash would like a nice Punjabi girl such as your Nikki for our family. We would like to request that she email him at the address we are providing below so that us parents can hear some good news soon. Regards, Singh family."

Contacting a random, unwitting involved guy to whom I came across as a weird stalker wasn't exactly good for the ego. I couldn't help but question where life had brought me during those times. Unfortunately, it happened often enough that most of us on these sites learned to protect what was left of our egos with some iteration of "Got your contact info from your parents (i.e., blame them, not me, for this random communication.) Hopefully, you were expecting this email (i.e., not blindsided, because if so, you have a huge battle on your hands. Don't shoot the messenger.)

Over time, I wised up a bit and inadvertently discovered a way out. It may not have lasted long, but it did buy me several months. For many of the boys' profiles he showed me, I chose "undecided" and said that I'd think about it. Obviously, this too got recorded in the notebook. When he'd remember to ask what I had decided regarding these profiles, I'd say that I was still thinking, and the issue would drop. Or so I thought. One day, Dad, fed up with the number of pending profiles, issued another decree. I could only say "yes" or "no" to a profile; no "I don't know" or "I'll think about it" any longer. Now you're probably thinking that should have been very easy. Metaphorically swipe left or right. But by now, you've surely, and quite accurately, concluded that in this arena, nothing was ever that simple.

Even to this day, I will say that deciding on someone based on a few facts and one or two pictures seems judgmental and somewhat harsh to me. But that was all the information I had, and was and still is, the premise of online dating. I'll be honest and say, there were those that right off the bat I knew were definitely not someone I could see myself with. Those I vetoed and Dad documented my response, given the apparently highly likely event that these transcripts would be requested for further review, making it clear, "case closed." Literally!

Unfortunately, saying "no" was not always that easy. Each "no" came with a litany of questions, particularly if Mom was even remotely a part of the proceedings.

"Why are you rejecting such a nice-looking boy?"

"He's a doctor."

"Everyone is going to become bald at some point."

"So what if he's short?"

"So what if his parents have requested your birth horoscope details? They're determining straight away, without wasting time, if things should proceed. If you let us, we would request the same information from all boys' parents."

Mom would continue with her devil's advocate reasoning and support for these random boys. If I said I wasn't attracted to a particular boy, she would disagree with my taste and then say, "Not everyone is photogenic. You can't judge based on a picture." Ironically, wasn't that exactly what I was being asked to do?

Mom had a counterargument for all my reasons to say no to a guy, and she made sure that I heard them. The battle was exhausting, and I often surrendered, "Fine, I'll consider him..." and Dad would diligently make his detailed notations. The notebook obviously needed constant updating.

The danger of such considerations was the barrage of follow-up questions they generated:

"Has the boy contacted you?" If I said no, they went into a flurry of excuses as to why, "Maybe our email to his parents didn't go through. Maybe they are in India and weren't able to give your contact details to their son yet. We'll try again."

If he did contact me, they wanted to know every detail of our conversation. "Has the communication been only via email, or have you two spoken on the telephone? Has he asked you to meet? Has any date and time been arranged? Why not? What are you waiting for? You're not getting any younger, you know." Clearly, with each passing second, I was putting a life of wedded bliss with a complete stranger at risk.

"You say you didn't think that the conversation was good? Why not? So what if there were awkward pauses, limited things in common to talk about, and uncomfortable silences? Some people are just not good at talking on the phone. You should meet him and give him a chance."

To try and convince me, they would say things like, "We've already talked with their parents, and the boy seems very nice. We told them that you would call and speak with him to set up a meeting. If you don't do so, it will mean our word was not honest, and that isn't right. What will they think of us? Also, it isn't nice to get another parent's hopes up. We have already committed. Don't you want to make us happy? Besides, if you don't try, you will never know. You don't lose anything. You only stand to gain. This is all happening for your benefit. One guy is all you need. We have a good feeling about this."

If anyone wants to learn the art of guilt-tripping, please see Indian parents. They are the foremost world's experts. This level of guilt and pressure proved too much to withstand, and consequently I, like many others in my shoes, caved.

Enter road two, the middle path, where there was mutual knowledge of one another, but not necessarily mutual desires and goals. That's only natural in any form of dating. It's just that here, the problem was compounded by the parental involvement factor, which, as you're starting to see, is a very powerful multiplier. When you're starting off meeting someone with such a baseline, your mind is, on some level, typically leaning towards *not interested*. I'm not saying that you couldn't have been pleasantly surprised, but that happening on both ends was pretty rare. It was even tougher when guys met with me just to appease their parents despite having zero interest in me, or maybe even the entire process. As if first dates weren't awkward enough.

Road three, the best-case scenario, where both the guy and I liked each other's profile and had a genuine interest in trying to get to know one another. It was such a pleasant sigh of relief when this happened. It was even enjoyable at times, especially when it seemed like there was real promise. Unfortunately, such a budding relationship was no match for the added pressure and hopes of parents that often squashed it prematurely. If it wasn't the constant inquiries as to the status of things, then it was being asked for horoscope details from the boy's parents to start planning the wedding after learning that one conversation had taken place. One spark of hope was all that was needed to light the wedding fire for many Indian parents.

So, these parents would try to "help" by communicating with Mom and Dad, provide unsolicited advice, and push for more meetings and finally, a decision. Of course, a favorable decision regarding the other person was the only one any parent wanted to hear. Anything else was too much to handle, and that waste of time in prime marriageable age years was a blow to their hearts that was often too much to take—and we were sure to hear about it for as long as we remained single.

As you can now clearly see, Indian online "dating" was far more than met the eye. One had to be in it to realize the depth of the issues in this pool, and I was in the deep end. Of course, I would have loved to climb out, drip-dry and never speak of the experience again, but that was not an option. While Mom and Dad agreed that it was wrong to waste anyone's time and energy, or to get anyone's hopes up without cause, they pointed out that not everyone was like this. There were still many good-intentioned, well-meaning boys and parents out there. I just had to continue to wade through the pool to find them. Mom and Dad didn't spend good money on swimming lessons so I could paddle around for a bit and eventually sink. If we were being honest—I wasn't allowed.

Quitting wasn't an option. There was no money-back guarantee on the subscription after all. Besides, I needed to toughen up and accept reality. Apparently, it's true what they say, all is fair in love and war, and this was war, alright—on my singledom—and Mom and Dad were winning this war one way or another, no ifs, ands, or buts about it.

Oh, and what about the "love" part of the saying? *Love only comes after marriage, obviously*. That's the sequel. Remember who we are after all.

Putting the Cart
Before the Horse

Not more than a few months had I been on this website, did the first battle between Mom, Dad and I occur. I like to refer to it as "premature does not equal maturity." I was home again for the weekend, after a recent trip to Siem Reap, visiting with them, and getting more than my fill of Mom's freshly made parathas. In retrospect, maybe I shouldn't have been visiting home so often.

"Beta, do you remember that photograph of the boy that I showed you?" asked Dad casually.

"No, not really," I replied. That must have been the answer that Dad had been expecting, because he pulled a picture out from a pile of papers sitting on the table next to him and handed it to me.

"This is the surgery resident from Florida. You said that you liked him." Glancing over at the picture of a guy in a suit with a professional background, I responded a bit matter-of-factly, "What I said was that he wasn't bad looking. That doesn't equate to me liking him, Dad. I don't even know him."

"Well, not to worry. We have a solution for that. His family had provided us with their telephone number and asked us to call them, so we did. Mom spoke with his mother, and their family would like to come here and meet you. Isn't that wonderful?" asked Dad, essentially rhetorically, as for him and Mom, there was no other possible answer but an emphatic "yes."

Sigh.

That was all I could muster at that moment. *How else was I to respond to that?* I would have loved to think that Dad was joking, but he wasn't even in the least. I would have also liked to tell you that I responded calmly and patiently, but that would have been a lie.

"What are you saying, Dad? Seriously, that's crazy! No, that's not great, it's ridiculous! Why would I want to meet this guy's parents when I haven't even met him? Absolutely not!"

"Beta, why are you getting so upset? What is wrong with his family wanting to meet you?" he asked, genuinely confused. *Oh, how much time did we have?* I should have known this battle was going to be a tough one (they all were)—but that did not stop me from fighting it. And fight a good fight I did, if I do say so myself.

"Dad, it makes no sense at all to spend time meeting some boy's family when I don't even know anything about this guy. I don't know whether or not he's normal, or if we'll get along. Will I like him? Will he like me? Will we even make it to being in a relationship? It's exactly like counting your chickens before they've hatched, and there's bound to be a dud or two. As for the meeting of families, we're talking about a point so far in the future when I haven't even spoken one word to this guy!"

"Beta, you're being completely unreasonable. Some parents like to get to know the family first, and there is nothing wrong with that," Mom chimed in.

"How does that make any sense? They want to know the family before we even know if that's necessary?" I asked.

"It makes complete sense. Knowing the family is very important. You want to marry a boy from a good family because when you get married, you don't just marry the boy, but also become part of their family." She would have liked to think she'd shut down any argument from me, but I was digging in.

"I understand that it's important to get to know the guy's family before you marry him, but at this point, it's beyond premature. We haven't even spoken once!" I was incensed, empowered, and equally surprised at my newfound ability to push back.

"Even if you don't think this is the way, which we don't understand at all, what is the big deal in meeting with them? What will you lose? It's just one day, and they have even agreed to come to our home. How will it harm you?" Dad asked.

They took strength in the power of a unified front and then began explaining how I should be more understanding and less judgmental of thought processes different from my own. They went into a lengthy speech about how marriages were previously arranged, and how this was a compromise of traditional and modern ways. Mom told me that I was being unnecessarily difficult and stubborn. She also informed me of how bad we all would look if she had to call and tell them not to come after she had already agreed to their request. Ahh, the good old "what would people think?" argument. Is there any situation to which it is not highly applicable?

The arguments and artillery kept coming. Just as it looked as though I was about to lose, in came my reserves. I loved having a brother who understood me and whom I could always count on. Like a relief pitcher at the bottom of the ninth inning with two men on and two men out,

Ayaan flew into the room with fresh energy and a will to win. He reiterated and stressed all the arguments regarding the futility of families meeting prior to the development of any sort of relationship. Given Ayaan's calm demeanor and relative impartiality, he made more of an impact on Mom and Dad. They finally accepted that I was not going to meet this boy's parents, and, disgruntled as they were, let the issue drop. *Homerun!*

Ah, the power of a fair fight.

Winning one battle was a far cry from success. I knew this, but like many others, I got caught up in the thrill of my victory. I also didn't actually realize at the time what success truly meant. I was twenty-two and clearly focused on the moment. At the time, I definitely didn't have perspective despite my temporary feeling of triumph. I'm a big kid now, so I can admit that.

I thought I had saved myself from potential suitors and their families. I thought I was free. Freedom was short-lived, however. Over the years that followed, many more such incidents occurred. They became more involved and consequential, and after Ayaan moved out to experience life living on his own, I was left fighting the losing battle alone for some time. It proved exhausting, and eventually I had no choice but to surrender.

I would come to learn the hard way that things don't always get easier with time.

When One Door Closes, Bang on the Others

T ime is the best and worst of solutions. Many times, its passing is long and arduous, like when trying to get over heartbreak. On the other hand, it's often regrettably swift in passing. It was oddly both in my situation. Residency is a tough phase of medical training, so having it go by as quickly as possible is pretty much every resident's desire. The first year and a half of residency had flown by, and I was thrilled. Mom and Dad? Not so much. Years, not days or months, had passed, and I was still single. Shockingly, the matrimonial online method had not produced results. The pages of the infamous notebook had become almost completely filled, and Mom and Dad were frustrated to say the least. It seemed like the title of the notebook would need to be changed from *"Nikki's God-Willing Prosperous Future"* to *"God, Does Nikki Even Have a Prosperous Future?"* Only a few pages left to find out.

The time to double down had come. Usually, when one method doesn't work, people try a newer, more novel approach. Mom and Dad, however, being old-school as they were, decided to employ old-school methods. If these tried and trusted methods had worked in the past, they would work now. Sure, it was a different country, another generation, and modern times, but what did that matter in the face of "old is gold"?

Their first go-to was the good old *word-of-mouth* method. Mom and Dad began by surveying all of their

46

friends for any potential marriage material. Any and all sons were eligible candidates.

"What about Arjun? You grew up with him. We know his family, and they seem interested in you." By *they*, Mom and Dad meant Arjun's parents. Arjun's opinion was obviously a very distant second. When I would protest and strongly express my disinterest, Mom and Dad would reluctantly move on to the next eligible bachelor. Having grown up with these men, I knew them enough to know that there were none that I was interested in from a dating or marriage perspective. However, my not being able to see their suggestions as potential life partners was a very difficult concept for Mom and Dad.

They didn't really understand it. Hence, they "moved on", foraging through single Indian guys in their prime like the cashmere clearance rack at Saks, but never letting go of any of the suggested men. Letting me know when a suitable "second" had been snatched up, taken to the altar, and bringing future doctors into the world, Mom would shoot me a side-eye, dejectedly reminding me, "That could have been you."

And the reminders were relentless:

"See? I told you to marry Arjun. Now look, he's marrying a lawyer. His fiancé doesn't care that he, what did you say, ' has a shiny bald head, and his breath smells like yesterday's coffee'. That's nothing that a few well-placed hair plugs and a bottle of Listerine couldn't remedy. Now, she is going to marry the only son of a nice and wealthy family and be his queen."

"Kavya's mom called to tell me that Amar is getting married next month. Apparently, he has lost a lot of weight since you two met, and now he has a successful business too. You rejected him and now look."

"Did you hear that Karan and his wife are having a baby? They are very happy together. See what could have been had you listened to me? But today's generation of children don't listen to their parents."

Why would it at all matter that those ships had sailed long ago? Or, that I had never wanted it to be me—and still didn't? In fact, that itself was the problem. That, and my not listening to Mom. These were crimes punishable for eternity. Somehow aging and forgetfulness do not apply when it comes to a mother's words not heeded. The only saving grace during these times was Dad, who would end such conversations by reminding us, aka Mom, that it was futile to revisit missed opportunities that were no longer a possibility. Mom would relent, but only until the next reminder of thwarted possibilities. Apparently, one *should* cry over spilled milk. If nothing else, cry enough and maybe the tears can fill the now empty glass back to half-full?

As you may surmise, this method worked for a very limited time, as Mom and Dad only knew a finite number of people with single sons for me to possibly marry, and I had "rejected them all" as they would say. However, this was a small, almost negligible hurdle in Mom and Dad's path. If they didn't personally know someone with an eligible son, that didn't mean others didn't. They started asking their friends about any eligible young men within their contacts. That was also a bit limited as they could only ask their friends who didn't have single daughters themselves because those parents would naturally be looking for matches for their own daughters first.

It did yield a few results, and one was from which "the incident" occurred. Mom and Dad's good friends had mentioned to them that a family that they knew who lived in a neighboring state had a son that appeared to be the perfect match. He was of similar age to me, a doctor, and from a nice family. Apparently, it was such a perfect match that Mom and Dad's friends arranged for the boy's family to come to their home and then "invited" Mom, Dad and I to their house at the same time so that he and I could meet in the company of all. *How fortuitous a coincidence!*

When Mom and Dad told me about all this on the auspicious meeting day, I was at a loss for words. When had we been transported back twenty-five years to India? When did trying old methods become literal replays of the past? Was I going to be asked to make and serve tea too? I obviously had no interest in being part of such an evening for so many reasons. First and foremost, the sheer awkwardness of the entire night was reason enough not to go. Second, the fact that he had agreed to come and participate told me everything I needed to know. If he was coming on his own volition, then he was likely too traditional a man for my taste. If he was coming by way of intimidation, then either he didn't have courage of his own convictions, or he was merely obliging his parents and thus not actually interested in meeting me.

I wanted no part in this meet and greet and adamantly refused. Mom and Dad, as you might have guessed, were extremely unhappy with my refusal. They tried everything from coercion, to pleading, to guilt, and finally the dreaded disappointment mixed with anger. When all failed and I did not acquiesce, they were left with no choice but to attend without me. They couldn't be late and come empty-handed after all. This may have been their only choice, but they certainly were not going to let the matter drop so easily. The sheer embarrassment of having to admit to having a disobedient daughter was one that they were not going to let me live down, not for many months to come.

"Do you even know how the family looked at us when we entered without you? When they asked where you were, we were forced to lie to save face! Everyone was very unhappy. What must our friends have thought about you not coming when they went to so much trouble to arrange the meeting? What must they have thought about us? What must the young man's parents have thought about us coming without you when their son came with them? Now our friends will never suggest any boys for you again! They may tell our other friends, and then they too may not suggest anyone for you. What will everyone think of you?!"

Those are just a few of the statements and observations Mom made over the next several days and weeks. The words may have varied, but the effect was the same—her efforts were only to ensure I understood the severity of her disapproval. In truth, Mom didn't actually have to say anything. Her look of disappointment that accompanied each stinging comment was enough to make me wonder how she, or I, would ever recover from such a dire event.

With the method of voluntary suggestions from Mom and Dad's friends on hold due to my disobedience, they were forced to pull out all the stops. If suitors were not going to come to us, then we'd have to find and go to them ourselves. The time to "sell" their daughter had come.

What is the best way to incite a sale? The same way you'd get rid of that old couch you no longer needed, or the unused treadmill you purchased that January you vowed to get into shape—put out an advertisement of course. Now, we were not wealthy enough to be able to obtain television advertising, but who needed that anyway when there was a reliable Indian newspaper in circulation. This was in physical print and therefore accessible to all ages and those who weren't good with computers. Furthermore, and most importantly, it was how their forefathers had arranged marriages, so it had a proven track record of success. Mom and Dad's confidence and hope received a much-needed boost.

An advertisement was quickly put together as the deadline for submission to appear in that week's distribution was fast approaching. *Hold on, does not haste make waste?* Mom and Dad had obviously not heard that saying, so it need not apply. Besides, creativity was not at all necessary. That's reserved for the liberal arts folks. Not us, who are factual math and science people. Basic information inputted into a winning formula clearly equals success, and who messes with that?

"North Indian Hindu parents seeking U.S.-born and raised physician for their twenty-three-year-old fair, slim, 5'4" beautiful, physician daughter," read my advertisement in that week's issue of the paper. Not only in that week's issue, but in the entire month's issues. Four weeks for the price of one was not only a fantastic deal, but more importantly, repetition is another key to success. That obviously must have been why at least ten other advertisements for other single women appeared almost identical to mine, give or take age or height if needed. With such a foolproof method, it seemed certain that success was just a stone's throw away.

Thank the gods, for they always open doors, even if they are back doors to the past.

Timing is Everything

I n our culture, destiny and fate are highly esteemed. There is the belief that we are born with a fate created by the result of past karma. Life unfolds according to this fate, and that is our destiny. There is also this concept that we mere mortals aren't the ones who do, but that it is God that is the ultimate doer of all. From this, one would then conclude that we believe that marriages are preordained. This in turn should lead to a sense of peace, knowing that it's all in God's hands, including when and to whom we get married. *Simple, right?* Not so fast.

Like many things in life, consistency is inconsistent. For a logical, science-oriented group of people who are also very religious, Indian parents somehow choose to follow neither road when it comes to the marriage of their children, particularly their daughters. In that case, it's all about action, and not at all the fun kind.

It was a warm summer weekend, about a month or so before my twenty-fourth birthday, and we were all sitting around the family room casually watching TV. Having joined the online dating—sorry, marriage—website, and with Mom and Dad employing all known techniques to get me married, there were very high hopes amongst them that one method or the other would yield fruitful results. In fact, they were convinced. Apparently, they were so convinced and confident that they felt the need to control and dictate the terms.

"Beta, you are not being serious," said Mom.

"About what?" I asked, confused, as I didn't think the melodramatic soap opera we were watching required anything more than limited attention. Clearly, to me, Mom's statement seemed to come out of nowhere, but as the concerned and loving parent she was, my future and I were always on her mind.

"You have been on this site for a couple of years already and we don't see you meeting many boys. You're either working, flying here or there in the world in your limited time off, or visiting us. Look, it's Saturday evening and you're sitting at home with us rather than out with a prospective boy. In fact, you are hardly even talking to any boys as far as we can tell. You just reject all of them. How will this work?"

Note to self: spending time with parents no longer makes you a good daughter.

"First of all, it hasn't been that long. Secondly, I actually enjoy spending time with you all, except of course when you're bothering me about things like this. Apparently, that's not mutual. Most importantly, though, I have plenty of time. I don't want to get married right now. I'm only twenty-three! Chillax!" Mom shook her head in horror, looked up to the heavens while mouthing aloud, "Only twenty-three?" and then, in complete exasperation, she turned to Dad, "What are we going to do with this girl?"

"Beta, we've already told you, we're not saying you have to get married tomorrow. But, if you aren't seriously meeting boys, then how will you possibly get married?" Dad chimed in now that he had been recruited to the conversation.

"Didn't you guys hear me? I have plenty of time!" I emphatically stated.

"Plenty of time? What nonsense are you speaking? It's the exact opposite! You already have wasted so much time," retorted Mom. "Do you hear her?" she turned to Dad, steeped in frustration.

Mom paused, took three deep breaths, and then, with as much calm restraint as she could muster, said, "Beta, that is not true. Time flies by without you even realizing. It passes so quickly, you won't even know where it went. Once it's gone, it doesn't come back! And we most certainly don't want the time to pass us by."

"What 'the time' are you talking about?"

"The right time to get married of course, beta, and that is just about upon us," answered Mom seriously.

"Wait, what?!"

"Nikki beta," said Mom in a tone implying that I was being infuriatingly naive, "the correct time to get married is between twenty-four and twenty-six years old. That's it! And you are dangerously close to that time," explained Mom with complete conviction. She may have thought this counted as an explanation, but it certainly did not for me.

When did God speak to Mom? Was this the only topic He or She had interest in discussing? Was He or She going to add this as the eleventh commandment? Or was this just a fad that should only be followed carefully and limitedly, lest you end up wearing painted-on jeggings in the new age of baggy boyfriend jeans? What happened if said decree was not followed? Would you fall off the edge of the earth on the first day of the twenty-seventh year of your life? *So many questions.*

"First of all, I'm too young to get married," I quipped back.

"Too young? Have you gone mad? You're talking totally silly now. In our times, girls were married and often had children by their early twenties," retorted Mom.

"We have already said that we are not asking you to get married tomorrow," repeated Dad, "we do, however, think that within the next three years is the right time to be married, and we must take steps towards that."

"Dad, when I said I was too young, I meant, now and also the next few years. I'm not ready to get married, and I don't see myself being ready within the next few years either. I still have many places around the world I want to visit and adventures I want to go on."

"Hai Ram," said Mom using the Hindi version of "Oh, God!" as she threw her hands in the air. "How can we put some sense into this girl?" she exclaimed.

"Nikki beta, we have lived and seen much more life than you, and we understand that there is a right time for everything, including marriage. And that time is between twenty-four and twenty-six. We're telling you, this is true," said Dad trying to restore calm amongst us.

"That's a ridiculously narrow timeframe—and way too soon!"

"It's neither soon nor ridiculous. You're the one being ridiculous. You might think you're not ready at this moment, but as you go through the process and meet someone, you will become ready," said Mom.

"No, my readiness doesn't depend on anyone else. I feel like I'm way too young, and just not yet ready for all that a marriage involves."

"You think that way now, but you will see. You will be. How could you not? It's the perfect time. You're young enough that you're not set in your ways and therefore compromise is not an issue, and also at the perfect age for children after marriage." I would have protested that portion, but if they didn't understand my lack of readiness to get married, they most certainly wouldn't understand my complete lack of readiness at that point in time for children.

"Why do I need to get married by twenty-six specifically? Why does it matter if it's beyond that?"

"'Beyond?' What are you saying beta? Hai Ram! Don't you see, once it gets too late, then it will be very difficult, if not impossible, to find any suitable boys? Then you'll be left all alone!" Mom paused, shuddering at the thought. "Also, there is a right time to have children. Do you want to have children after more than a third of your life has gone? Does that even make sense? Why don't you understand?"

"There is a lot of time between twenty-six and then. Marriage doesn't have to happen within that window. I don't know why you both can't see that."

"Beta, it's very important to find a partner at the right time. Having a partner who will be with you throughout life, even when we are gone, is very important." *Did we really need the "dying" guilt added into the mix?*

I felt backed into a corner. The united front was fierce, making me want to flee faster than a cheetah on the hunt. That's when I said it, the word—"I'll think about it when I'm thirty!" My mother's eyes widened so big it seemed like she had forgotten how to blink, "Thirty?!!!" I thought she'd pass out. "Thirty?!!!" she repeated. You would have thought I'd let loose a stream of curse words. She approached me, finger extended and shook it near my nose. "Do not *ever* say that when it comes to your future as a married woman! Do you hear me?" Dad stepped in calmly, but sternly, "That's enough of this." He turned to me, "Fine, we'll compromise, since unlike you, we understand its value very well. We're married after all. We will accept marriage up to age twenty-seven, but *that's it!*"

Completely flabbergasted, Mom returned to her cooking, indicating the conversation was over. Apparently, that was their best and final offer. Take it—or take it. Besides, apparently, this was extreme generosity on their part, and if I couldn't see that, then the fault was obviously mine. I wanted to ask why Ayaan got a pass on these parental decrees, seemingly reserved for daughters who apparently, regardless of grades, framed diplomas, and ambitions, had only one life mission—marriage, to a doctor or engineer of Indian descent, accomplished between the ages of twenty-four and begrudgingly, twenty-seven, but I knew better.

Fast forward to a few months after my twenty-seventh birthday. I was bringing home the guy that I had been seriously seeing to meet my parents! It was a day that they had been losing hope of seeing, so of course, they were beyond elated. Words cannot do their revival and happiness justice. It was the moment Mom and Dad had dreamed, prayed, and impatiently waited too long for—meeting their likely son-in-law. Nothing could have been sweeter for them. They were on cloud nine.

Years later, Mom would tell me how around that time, she would repeatedly thank God for answering her prayers that her daughter be married by twenty-seven. *Hallelujah, just in the nick of time!* Dangerously close but saved from falling off the 'edge of the Earth'! God is truly merciful.

Unfortunately, that meeting proved to be like a flash of lightning, bringing momentary bright light, but followed by deafening thunder. Soon after the fateful dinner, the guy got cold feet and disappeared, ghosting me before ghosting was a thing. If only I had started writing then, I could have coined the term and at least gained more than heartbreak. Thank God though that the world is round and not square, for I lived another day to tell this story. Turns out, people say and use all those cliches for a reason—they're apparently totally true. You make plans or hardline dictums in the case of Mom and Dad, and God really does laugh—and apparently, timing *is* everything.

Let's Get Back to Science
Cue the Stars

I ndians are interesting people. Our TV shows, or serials, as they are popularly known, are over the top melodramatic displays of emotion. We don't hold back when it comes to making our opinions known. Yet, when it comes to actually expressing our innermost thoughts and feelings, we hide those like Kohinoor diamonds that we don't want taken from us—*fool me once, shame on you, fool me twice, shame on me*—the saying goes. And we're all seeing how eerily accurate those people with all the sayings are.

This whole process of "finding someone" was starting to feel very much like homework. I know I'm supposed to love extra credit work and all, but earning these brownie points wasn't feeling like a treat. Maybe that's why I "wasn't serious." I really did want to find someone, but I wanted that someone to meet me on the road. And if we could meet on the road to a Trevor Noah or Hasan Minhaj stand-up comedy show, even better. Meeting someone was supposed to be enjoyable. Or at least that was the bubble I was living under. Too bad my parents were constantly trying to burst my bubble with their reality of hard work. *Reality bites.* Yet again, the cliche is true! Why am I still surprised?! Clearly, I had learned nothing from the amazing observational skills of my two favorite comedians.

It was tedious, exhausting and confusing . Take the advice I'd receive. "You'll meet someone when you're not looking and least expecting it," my married friends would say while advising me to focus on other things. *Huh? Okay, so, do nothing?* Then while I was heeding such wisdom, I'd get thrown off my ass, with the "No one is going to magically fall into your lap. You need to look seriously and actively put yourself out there," advice given to me by my parents and all the supposedly wiser relatives and family friends in my life.

Get to "work" and when I still didn't find anyone, friends like Kavya would help with, "You're trying too hard. That can give off an air of desperation and may not attract and keep the right kind of guy." *Okay, be cool. Just take it easy.* Then Mom would catch me "loafing" around, and advise, "Beta, you need to hurry up and pick someone from the options that exist and just get married now. All marriage is about adjustment, hard work, and compromise anyway. That's why arranged marriages worked." I studied her face, agreed, she and Dad were good for one another, and equally good for Ayaan and me, but had she felt the pulls at her heart, or the wildly breathless moments she loved to watch in her serials? Did she know the exhilaration of a heart-pounding romance? It was like I was the insane one, just wanting to have the most important relationship of my life be more than a contract of convenience.

Okay, note to self, get serious now. Cue friends, like Divya, "You're putting too much pressure on yourself and this. Marriage is not a destination. If it happens, that's great. If it doesn't, that's okay too. Enjoy the process." A little whiff of this, and Mom would say, "What nonsense. The people who are married themselves are saying this to you? It applies to you but not them? Beta, it is something that we work for because having a partner, the right partner, is very important in life."

A girl is going to get whiplash! Can you all convene, have a meeting of the minds, and when the winning strategy emerges, call me. I'll be yo-yoing back and forth until then, thanks.

I know everyone meant well, and I appreciated them all. Clearly, no one had the answer, but it seemed like very few of them realized that. Married friends seemed to love to impart advice as if they'd found the holy grail, but it often seemed to me like it just so happened that luck and timing had collided, and life had worked out in this matter for them.

Sure, Kavya met her husband in a club, but I had gone to clubs and didn't come away with the same goody bag. Not all club experiences are created equal; some are rich in champagne glasses and sparklers, while others are littered with empty red cups and equally empty promises. My parents genuinely cared, and they came from the best place, but they didn't know anything other than hard work. It was what had led to their success in all aspects of their lives, and this was no different to them. Plus, they had never dated or gone through this themselves, so their advice was secondhand.

So, it seemed that neither firsthand experience from married friends nor secondhand advice from parents and relatives seemed to be the glass slipper of strategies. It was definitely frustrating at times. And honestly, disheartening too. I agreed, marriage was not a destination. It was not *the* source of happiness but should add to existing happiness from within. But I also agreed that being married was important for me. I wanted a partner with whom I could share life's ups, downs, joys, sadness, challenges, and triumphs. I agreed that putting too much pressure on it was futile, but also agreed that looking, trying, and putting myself out there was important. I just didn't know how to achieve that oh-so-unattainable balance.

So, I continued to listen and try all of the advice of the caring, well-meaning people in my life. Listened, and eventually concluded that it was all about the Universe, timing, and destiny. You could do x, not do x, try y, not try y, or put all your eggs in the z basket, but one was not necessarily better than the others. It was scary and comforting all at the same time, freeing me to focus on myself, my work, and my passion for traveling and experiencing the world far and wide.

To me, it just seemed like when the stars aligned, it would happen, literally and metaphorically. I am Indian after all, and the power of astrology goes way back with our people.

Plus, astrology is a science according to my people. And science doesn't have contradictions. It's black and white, and often brown.

No Bad Language

Ahh, summer.

The best time of the year. As children, the sheer joy experienced from being off from school for a whole two months was an unparalleled feeling. We loved it, we enjoyed it, but we didn't always appreciate it. We often couldn't. Two months felt like an endless and expansive time period. Actually, remove the word *period* after the word time, as that would imply limitation to the time, and we did not comprehend any parameters in the glorious days of sun and freedom.

As adults, we generally still enjoy summer. We revel in the noticeably lighter traffic, the ability to see the sun as we travel to and from our jobs, and the lingering happy hours that become dinner and drinks. And just like children, we too do not fully appreciate summer. We don't have that unbridled joy or sense of freedom that we did as children because work and responsibility don't allow us a summer holiday at a beach house. We may take a short vacation for a week at the beach, enjoying the Saturday of driving, shopping, exploring our surroundings, and eating fresh seafood. But by Wednesday, thoughts of those quintessential duties of adulthood have crept into our heads, and we're already dreading the packing, the cleaning, that long drive home to tackle hundreds of emails and a looming work calendar starting with a jam-packed Monday. It's adulting at its ugliest.

So, why these serious contemplative thoughts, you ask? Because I was an adult who had the opportunity to be a child again. To bask in the gloriousness of the unbridled, unrestricted, mind-boggling days and months of abandon that lay before me. I had four whole months off after finishing my fellowship and before starting my job! What was I going to do with all this time? *Absolutely nothing!*

That's the thing about freedom, there are no rules, plans, or itineraries. No panic-filled mornings awakening to the blare of the alarm clock at 6:00 am, only to hit the snooze button—not once, but twice. What followed was a mad dash to the shower while simultaneously pulling my head of unruly curls into a bun to be "ready," jumping into a blue collared shirt and brown dress pants interchangeable "outfit," grabbing a container of yesterday's leftovers and speeding to work to arrive by 7:00 am to begin a 13-hour day where a five-minute break to eat said leftovers while pretending to be in the bathroom awaited.

The first Monday of freedom found me awake at 7:00 am. I tried convincing myself that I was dreaming and therefore still asleep, but after 10 minutes of tossing and turning, I finally realized I wasn't easily convinced and climbed out of bed. And what did I do next? Check my email! *Even though I wasn't working!*

Now, I understand that for the vast majority of people with internet, that's the norm. But anyone who knew me—or knows me, shall I say (some things never change), understood that they needed to text me to inform me that they'd sent me an email, and then call me a few days later to hopefully get a reply.

I was obviously one of those who were reluctant to get a smartphone for the longest time as having email available 24/7 was way too much pressure for me. I protested for as long as I could and then realized that if I didn't cave, along with being an old soul internally, I would be an even older soul technologically—and that was already bordering on ancient. I'm talking Pangea times.

Upon opening my email, the first thing that popped up was a message from my former co-fellow and great friend joyously informing me that it was 7:00 am and we were not at work. Old habits fade slowly. That was also my record for fastest opening and reading of an email to date. It was such a momentous feat, I decided it was not worth trying to replicate ever again, as such greatness is only achieved but once in a lifetime.

I digress. And really, I should back up a little and tell you how I had come to have all this time off. I had just completed my two-year fellowship. Yes, I may seem like a bit of an overachiever, but really, I was just a mere achiever in the world of medicine. It's so ubiquitous in this profession that most accomplishments often seem like an underachievement unless the said achievement rises above the ground of us mortal MDs and reaches the stars of university, state, country, and/or world renown.

Anyway, I had just completed my fellowship and was waiting to start my first job. Contracts had been signed, endless paperwork finalized, and the last of certifying exams passed and completed for a decade. There was no foreseeable responsibility or studying of any kind for me *for the next four months*! It was too glorious a feeling to put into words. It was a sense of calm, peace, liberation, and ease that I had not felt in the longest time. I could not only enjoy my time in the true sense of the word, but also my upcoming birthday.

The big 3-0... I really never imagined myself being thirty. It had always seemed like such a distant point in time that, somehow in my mind, I didn't think the day would ever actually be upon me. Yes, I'm an old soul, but my old soul is in juxtaposition to a forever teenager. Freely dancing around my parents' house, which I still to this day refer to as home no matter where I actually live or have lived, coming to their bed when I get home late at night to gossip with Mom about the evening's events, and touching the bald spot on the top of Dad's head with my forever cold hands causing him to jump while man-squealing, are all normalities for me. This all the while being a responsible individual who follows all the rules, and a physician caring for patients with serious conditions. As I mentioned, I'm an old young person.

Turning thirty is a big deal. It's the start of a new chapter that brings with it increased maturity, wisdom, and stability. It also brings with it the opportunity to explore avenues created from said stability. For me, it was the start of a decade of many firsts. I would begin my first real job. Yes, I had worked, and worked hard, the last several years, but it had all been training. It was education, followed by education in the form of on-the-job training, and then by more specialized on-site training. It all led to finally being able to practice medicine without a captain. Up until this point, I had always been somewhere in the line of command, slowly moving up towards the number one spot, but not quite reaching there until now. This job would signify the actualization of becoming first in charge. Done being a supporting character, I would finally become the star of my show. It was daunting and exciting.

This decade would also be the start of leisure incorporated into life. I don't want to keep harping on details of the difficult and long road of medical training, but it had left me with time for little else. I started college before high school even finished. Yes, really. You see, the college program I had the privilege of attending (I can say that now) began its summer classes before my high school graduation. So, I obtained permission to leave high school early and begin summer school. College summer school, so obviously it was cooler and better, and therefore made up for missing the last few weeks of idling around high school hallways, reminiscing over the last four years. Besides, as Mom told me when I asked her why she wasn't excited like all the other parents at my high school graduation ceremony, which I did come back for, there was nothing to be particularly excited about at that point. She would only be excited at my medical school graduation—when I had accomplished something. For her, like many other first-generation immigrant parents, high school graduation was akin to buying groceries. You obviously got the ingredients before indulging in a fabulously prepared meal—and no one celebrates the food shopping.

Once the train left the platform, it didn't quite stop for the next twelve years. Three semesters later and year one of my two-year college stint was complete. Summer arrived and brought with it a full-time study program for the MCATs, or Medical College Admissions Test, capped off by the actual examination, which I was required to pass. Some people spend the last weekend of summer at the beach. Me? The chilly interior of a testing center.

Then, as expected after "summer break," it was back to school for year two of college. While this sounds like all work and no play, I did enjoy myself along the way.

New friends, new experiences, and my favorite—study abroad. It hadn't been done in my program, but I figured out an arrangement to make it happen. Granted that did mean my having to take twenty-one credits, of which fifteen were in science, the semester before, but clearly, it had already been carved into my mind by Mom and Dad that anything "worth it" required lots of work and sacrifice.

The train then continued on to four years of medical school, one year of internship, three years of residency, and two years of fellowship. During each phase, I spent many a day wishing for the completion of that step and the moving on to the next. I was in a self-induced race to a shingle with my name followed by the much-sought-after M.D., my parents' look of pride in their only daughter's accomplishment, and my own sense of satisfaction in completing the arduous road to becoming not just a neurologist, but a subspecialized critical-care neurologist. The only thing was, in this long race to the finish, wishing away each step in my quest to the next, I had essentially wished away my twenties. Don't they say those are some of the best years of our lives? I guess I didn't get that memo. Should've checked my email.

"When you wish upon a star, makes no difference who you are, anything your heart desires will come to you." Apparently, I was doing a hell of a lot of stargazing during my twenties. And apparently, wishes do come true…here I was bidding adieu to my twenties and saying hello to my thirties. Fitting those lines were from Pinocchio… *Should have used my powers a bit more wisely*. But alas, it was too late. The moment was here, and I was ready to embrace this new phase of life—sort of. But first, I was ready for the grand celebratory party that would mark this milestone occasion in my life. After all, you only turn thirty but once in a lifetime. It's not like twenty-seven, which comes annually thereafter.

I know, coming from an independent woman who—aside from immediate family—relies on no one, this is probably going to sound regressive, backward, contradictory, and possibly even just plain silly, but I had always wanted to be thrown a birthday party by *someone*. I had wanted *someone* to surprise me with a mega-bash with all my friends, good music, dancing, champagne, and most importantly, my true love—a not-too-sweet, delectable, scrumptious dark chocolate cake. Trite, cliché, but so damn good.

If *someone* were to throw another a birthday party, it would be for a special birthday year, and mine had arrived. The desire was there, and the timing was right. Everything was perfect, save for one very minor detail—the *someone* to actually host the said celebration. Typically, such responsibility, or honor, depending on how you see it, falls to a significant other. And there lay the problem. You see, I was still single. Shocking for you all, I'm sure.

So, without a significant other from which to have such simple expectations, responsibilities to meet said expectations fell to the one person who was to be counted on, and fortunately, or unfortunately, again depending on how you saw it, required to solve all of my life's woes—Mom. She had always been the best. No matter what I needed, how many times I fell, or what support I required, she was always there. She was always a beacon of consistency and love. So, logically, she would step up this time like all others.

In this, my logic failed. Not because I had misjudged, but because I had ignored my accurate assessment, and therefore facts. Her behavior was exactly what I had said earlier it had always been—consistent. She was true to herself, and for that, I'd like to give her credit and say that I absolve her completely, but not enough time has passed for me to have grown so mature and wise.

By now, you may have guessed, said party did not occur. Far from my envisioning of grandeur was reality. You see, my birthday came and went, and yes, my family and most friends did remember and wish me a happy birthday, but they went about their lives on that Tuesday like every other day. It was a day no different from the previous or the one after. Understandably, a weekday was no evening to have a party, so I waited through the following Friday and Saturday to no avail—and with that avail came no friends, no champagne, no dancing, and no glorious chocolate creation. Now, before I begin to sound like a bratty child full of first-world problems, let me tell you that my feelings of disappointment ran much deeper.

When I brought it up with Mom, I was more than a bit upset, which was not entirely her fault. I had let my ire simmer for a good five days, and the pot was ready to blow. I raised the subject of the "non-party," prepared to resist accepting her profuse apology for as long as possible. Instead, I was on the receiving end of a blow that would knock the wind out of me and leave me momentarily dazed. "Nikki beta, what would we be celebrating? Our still single daughter turning thirty without any marriage prospects and future in sight? This is not something to be happy about. In fact, the last thing we want to do is bring attention to all of this." See what I mean? *POW!* This virtual punch to the nose and gut flattened me like an inflatable kiddie clown stuck in a horizontal state. I guess, *who would celebrate when you are mourning the falling off the edge of the world by your daughter?*

Various cultures mourn deaths for various time frames. Indians traditionally mourn for either the subsequent thirteen or forty days. In this aspect, Mom bucked tradition and mourned in front of the shrine to my lost youth for so long that I lost track of time. I guess traditions are meant to be selectively chosen.

Mom didn't mourn in the traditional sense—it was a new age after all, but she did go through the stages of grief. Some stages lasted longer than others. In her case, the first stage of denial was the longest of them all. That summer, a few weeks after my birthday, we went to a gathering at a family friend's home. All of Mom and Dad's close friends were there, and as usual, they had many questions—and even more advice—for us "children." An uncle, the term we use to describe any and every male older than us, whether we shared a bloodline or not, had cornered me into one of those quintessential conversations that I was always obliged to respectfully participate in, but internally loathed.

"So have you found anyone yet?" asked this uncle. My first instinct was to make a run for it—I knew this drill all too well. My career accomplishments would be set aside by yet another member of the patriarchy to focus on my failure to lasso a husband and begin my search for the latest and greatest in baby paraphernalia. Wildly, it wasn't just the men. The "Aunties" were even nosier and more consumed with "solving" the dilemma of spinsterhood.

There are so many things wrong with that question— *where do I begin?*

First, if I were seeing someone, why would I care to tell a person who is neither my close friend nor family? Hell, I may not even want to tell those people at times. Second, why is this uncle or aunty even asking? Does it affect his or her life in any way? Does he or she truly care about the answer? No—well then, that just makes it idle curiosity and thus gossip, or in my opinion, a shallow point of discussion. Third, the "yet" at the end of the question implies that the time taken for such an endeavor of finding a spouse has gone on too long—clearly beyond the realm of acceptability, and more importantly, beyond the uncle or auntie's level of patience. Life must be so frustrating for them, having to inquire so much. I wanted to carry around a stack of cards to hand out in these painful situations. They would be entitled "5 Points to Understand to Break Your Asking '*The Question*' to a Single Woman Bad Habit":

1.   Taking a spouse or being with a significant other isn't a requirement, but a choice, and something not everyone chooses.

2.   A person is not incomplete or somehow lacking without a significant other. Internal happiness and fulfillment should come from within and be independent of others.

3.   It has the potential to hurt the self-worth of a person, particularly someone who has not yet internalized point number two.

4.   What is the goal of life? Does anyone know? I sincerely hope and believe that there is more to life's purpose than "finding someone," but I'm no guru and I certainly don't have all the answers.

5.   If finding a significant other is something that someone wants for themselves in his or her life, and they haven't, then such repeated questions essentially serve to remind and thus frustrate and/or upset such individuals. This is even truer if it turns out it *is* the goal of life.

In response, I wanted to say, "Yes, this gorgeous, brilliant, successful, amazing nonexistent man standing next to me is my husband," but such a bold move would surely get back to my parents, and I would forever be blamed for the death of their social lives. So, I just said "no." Well, as they say, no good deed goes unpunished, so I got mine—a diatribe from my uncle that started with, "You really need to be serious and find someone before you turn thirty, because once you do, after that, it becomes extremely difficult." There just isn't a sigh long enough…

Luckily for me, he didn't stop there. This sixty-five-year-old uncle gave me suggestions and tips on how and where to land a husband as if there were "Single Men Boutiques" and a lecture on avoiding the lonely, inescapable life that awaits in spinsterhood. Just as I thought I was going to burst from all the joy that was this speech (I don't want to use the word conversation because that would imply there were two people speaking), a ray of hope appeared. Mom came and stood by me. My savior to prevent the imminent explosion.

"I was just telling your daughter that this is the right and high time to find someone, otherwise it becomes impossible," said the uncle to Mom. Mom nodded in agreement and said, "I tell her the same thing, too." Some savior.

"How old is your daughter by the way?" he asked in hushed tones.

Mom paused, looked at me and then down, stammered for a second, and then said, "twenty-nine."

"Oh! That is very tough, but there's still a little time. Just not too much. Don't wait any longer. After thirty, there are very few, if any, boys left," said the uncle.

As you can likely surmise, I was surprised, puzzled, enraged, and a bit hurt. Yet again, so many things wrong that I don't know where to begin. So, I won't even get into it—just reference above.

That was the day that I learned that thirty really is a dirty word. Shameful, embarrassing, and not to be spoken in polite company. And as Dad had taught us our entire lives, "No bad language."

Picky Sue

Y ou're too picky." That's what I've been told by Mom and Dad, their friends, my relatives far and wide, and just about anyone who hears that I'm unmarried. Unsolicited advice is super desirable, no?

Is there really such a thing as "too picky" when it comes to such a monumental decision as choosing a life partner? Apparently, the answer is a resounding "yes" if you ask Mom and Dad. Whenever I would return from a first date, Mom would eagerly ask how it had gone. In the beginning, I would describe the small and large things that turned me off of the guy.

"He wore a bubble vest and Crocs to dinner."

"He only drank tea, without anything in it, because everything else on the menu was not part of his food regimen, which, according to him, kept him looking much younger than his friends his age. Oh, and he wouldn't travel to places like Italy because he doesn't eat pasta on this diet."

"He spent the whole night talking about medicine and didn't seem to have any other interests."

"He asked to split our $15 bill, and then said, 'I'll pay $8, and you can pay the remaining $7' as if that was massive generosity on his part!"

"At the end of the lunch, he asked me to come see his car. If bragging about his BMW wasn't bad enough, he pointed out the license plate, which read 'Dr 90210". When I sarcastically commented that I was surprised no one else had such a plate, he seriously told me how he had custom-ordered the license plate after temporarily living in California for only one year!"

Pretty much anything I said that was not in favor of my going on a second date with said guy had Mom telling me that I wasn't giving him a chance in so many ways. "Some guys get nervous and are not good at dates"; that I was reading too much into small things, that x-y-z wouldn't matter in the future, or that said grievances were actually "not a big deal".

If I didn't know better, I'd say she had a side gig as a hired advocate for my dates, who, by the way, she knew almost nothing about. She certainly missed her calling as a lobbyist for young men in search of wives. It reminded me of when we were children and would get into trouble at school. Just like now, we were always wrong, and the other, then the teacher, was always right.

Noting the defense strategy I would have to mount to explain my reason for not wanting to go on a second date with a guy, I changed my tactic. I decided to be broader in my responses and answer truthfully that he wasn't for me because there wasn't chemistry between us. This created another ball of wax. Explaining the concept of chemistry to Mom turned out to be even harder than explaining dating, which was odd given the fact that Mom was a chemical engineer. "What is this chemistry business? You think you will just like someone right away? That's not how things work," she'd say. *Hmm, that was odd considering that arranged marriages, including hers, were based on the premise of liking, or not, the other person in one meeting!*

Regardless of which explanation I gave as to why there would be no second date, the outcome would be the same—Mom's face would fall, and I could almost hear her heart breaking in utter disappointment. It didn't help that Ayaan would inevitably enter stage left and pile on to the mound of stress with sayings like, "The one date wonder at it again?" Clearly, he had nothing better to do and enjoyed my suffering way too much. Mom was not one to take "no" easily. She obviously felt it was her duty to convince me otherwise. Mothers always know best after all.

"Beta, you know that a perfect person does not exist, right? You are nowhere near perfect, and you cannot expect others to be."

"Thank you, Mom. I'm well aware. I'm not looking for perfection. I'm looking for someone with whom I have compatibility and chemistry."

"Beta, you can't have everything."

"Who said I want everything?"

"Good-looking, tall , doctor, smart, this, that. Nobody has everything. You think the guy should be a model but looks don't matter. You should be looking for a nice boy from a good family. That is what is important."

"Who said anything about wanting a model? I want someone who I think is good-looking, but that by no means equates to the guy being a model. If he happens to have model good looks, well, that would just be a sweet bonus. And I do want a nice guy. I just want to be attracted to him."

"As you get older, you will realize, looks don't matter and are not important at all. You will see that they serve no real purpose. It's what type of person he is that matters. You are young and focusing on the wrong things."

"I totally disagree." One thing I learned from Mom over the years was the ability to dig my heels in when I felt I was right. The problem arose when we found ourselves on opposite sides of the fence.

"That is because you are not our age and haven't the experience we do."

"Look, I don't think I will ever feel that looks are completely unimportant. But for argument's sake, let's say that when I'm your age, they won't matter to me. But why can't I want and enjoy them now? It's like telling a child not to enjoy any of the aspects of childhood since childhood will pass."

"Beta, you don't understand my point, as you are not my age." Mom then tried a different approach to reach her goal. "You see that Jaya auntie's daughter Tina's husband is not good-looking, and she is very happily married. In fact, Jaya aunty was saying it's better for girls to find a husband who is not good-looking because such men will treat a girl better. They will make better husbands, and you'll be happier. You should really think about that. It makes complete sense, and I very much agree with her."

I considered bringing her argument up with Dad and shifting the conversation between us to one between them. *Was Dad not good-looking? Did he know her feelings about a partner's looks and appearance?* Hmmm, it did feel powerful to have "nuclear" codes in my pocket. However tempting, I resisted.

How had we gone from me wanting to be with a model to now needing to find an *ugly* guy?

"I definitely don't agree with that. And I don't understand why you seem to think that I can't have both.

Why can't I find a good-looking guy who is also nice, and with whom I'm happy? There are lots of people who have found such husbands. Why can't I be one of them? You always tell me to think positively and have hope and faith. So why can't I apply that here?"

"Beta, that's not how it works," said Mom. *Oh, really?* Apparently, Mom had all the answers, and hope and faith were incorrect ones in this arena. Interesting, since I had thought they covered all genres. I'll have to remember to tell God about this when he questions my selective faith.

"Nobody has everything, and there is no perfect man. In fact, you should be very happy if you get seven out of ten things you are looking for. You should consider yourself very lucky in such a case."

"Wait, are you seriously telling me that seventy percent is now good? That it's desirable and aspirational? So, when it comes to the most important aspect of my life, choosing a life partner, seventy percent is now more than totally fine, yet in school, anything less than 100% was unacceptable?"

I had no words. This was the same woman who, when I would come home with a 96% on a test, would ask where the other four points were. Why had I left some points on the table?

When I got well into the seven hundreds on each section of the SATs, rather than being elated, she had been despondent that neither score had been the full eight hundred! But now, all of a sudden, seventy was "good" in life? Clearly, I had had all my priorities backward. I had thought that a spouse, marriage, and personal happiness were some of the most important aspects of life.

Apparently, I really was naive. More like foolish. No wonder I only got 96%.

Age is Not Just a Number

W hen asked our age as children, we were often very specific, making sure to inform the questioner about the number of months that had already elapsed since our last birthday. "I'm seven and a half," we would announce with pride. Then somewhere along the way, we'd lose the half and cling desperately to our current age until the stroke of midnight nudged us a little closer to the next looming decade. Eventually, life comes full circle, and the months once again become essential in branding us as successful in the game of life, "I'm eighty-four and eight months."

That in-between stage is the tough period. We anticipate 21, turn 30, hit 40—the older we get, the more violent the milestones become. We often feel younger than we are, and they say age is just a number, so why can't we be carefree, choose an age we fancy, and stick with it? We have a favorite food, a favorite pastime, why not a favorite age?

"I like 27 best. I'm looking to purchase a condo right here," we'd say, happily settling in. Why can't this work? Because we're Indian girls of marriageable age, that's why. Such leeways do not apply to us. And what's even more unfortunate is that "age" can be an expansive time period. But just like milk, cross that date, and you'll be expired and likely soured.

Years had passed since I was placed on the dating site, and both Mom and Dad were getting worried. Initially, it had been just Mom who had panicked.

"Aren't you worried that Nikki isn't married yet?" Mom asked while sharply nudging my snoring dad, who was sleeping beside her. She nudged him several more times to finally get a "What?" from rightfully confused Dad, wondering what was happening in the middle of the night.

"Isn't the thought of our over thirty-year-old single daughter keeping you up? It's definitely not letting me sleep," said Mom exasperatedly as she looked over at the clock, reading 2:15 a.m.

"You know I don't worry about things. Everyone has their own fate. Now go to sleep and let me do the same," said Dad as he rolled over and nodded off.

I guess many such interrupted, poor-sleep nights got to Dad, because he soon joined the concerned bandwagon. Now, I won't say he ever panicked or stressed, because he doesn't do those things regarding anything in life. But he did develop increasing levels of concern over time, and this, like most things from parent to child, was passed onto me.

"Nikki beta, I think you need to loosen your criteria to broaden your potential prospects," said Dad to me one day. "Beta, you're past thirty now, and prospects are very few in your age range. And with each passing year, they continue to grow smaller. The number of eligible boys is already so low that if you don't consider those you may not have in the past, how will you get married?"

"Dad, what do you want me to do?" I asked impatiently, knowing that yet another painful conversation was about to ensue.

"I think we should consider non-doctors. There are many other good professions," said Dad.

Really? When did those turn up?

I'm pretty sure there were only two, doctors and engineers, because growing up, I heard of no others. And, according to every aunty and uncle I knew, doctors were atop the hierarchy of the only two professions one could be as an Indian child. Times—they were a'changing.

Mom heard this and scowled. She had always embraced the mindset that a female doctor should marry a male doctor. They'd understand ungodly work hours, be able to talk shop over dinner, and mingle at "doctor" parties with equal prestige.

"What are you saying? If she marries a doctor, then he too will understand the path of medicine, its difficulties, and requirements. Besides, so many non-doctor girls are finding and marrying doctors, so why can't our daughter? I say again, she should compromise in the looks department," added Mom. She was looking at Dad as though the discussion concerned only the two of them. I was once again invisible.

"I know many girls are finding doctors, but our daughter has not found one, and time is passing. She must consider other professionals," said Dad matter-of-factly.

"The best time to find someone is in school. Everyone agrees. Seema aunty, Naina aunty, Reema aunty—all of their daughters met their husbands in school," Mom remarked. Did she forget that ship had sailed several years ago?

"First of all, that's luck if someone you like happens to be in school with you. You know medical school classes are small, so options are limited. Second, what is the point of that statement when I've been done with school for years now?" I quipped.

"There were boys, and I told you then, like I'm telling you now. But you didn't listen, and look!" said Mom, throwing her hands up in frustration.

"Calm down. What has passed is passed. We can't change that, so let's not speak of it any further. Let's come back to the topic we were discussing," said Dad, trying to redirect the conversation.

"I'm fine with meeting non-doctors and have met several already. They just weren't for me," I informed Mom and Dad. They—largely Dad—seemed satisfied with my agreement to this first broadening of my prospect circle, that they didn't bother commenting on the fact that I hadn't told them of these dates, or that I had "rejected" so many candidates for life-partners.

This was only the start of the enlargement of my prospect circle. With each passing year, and/or couple of months, and my not getting any younger, Mom and Dad found a new desire of mine that they felt needed to be shed. The "doctor" one caused Mom more pain than me, since that desire had been one that had largely emanated from her and Dad. For the rest of the "criteria", I was essentially on my own and would receive little support from either one of them when I tried to hold on.

In the very early days, I had wanted a guy whose family came from the same region of India as mine. This was very common among Indians. Gujaratis preferred to marry Gujaratis, Punjabis preferred to marry Punjabis, and so on. People from different regions of India vary significantly in food, dress, language, and even culture, so much so that marrying someone of a different subgroup was almost akin to marrying a non-Indian. Thus, it was common for Indians to seek someone from a similar regional background.

That luxury was obviously one that, when I was younger with more "potentials," could have possibly been afforded to me, but was no longer even a remote consideration. I would say, surprisingly, Mom and Dad gave up on this sooner than I did, but desperate times called for desperate measures after all. Mom would initially tell me things like "Forget North Indian boys. South Indian boys are much nicer. People say they make good husbands." That eventually evolved into, "All you need is a nice boy from a good family. Doesn't matter what he is. Just get married." I agreed that the subgroup of Indian didn't matter and gave up on it pretty quickly myself. Giving up on wanting to marry an Indian guy, however, took longer and substantial coaxing by my family and friends. I had wanted someone who would naturally understand all that I had been through in trying to find him. I soon came to realize that only other single Indian women would truly understand, and they weren't who I was seeking, so giving up that notion only made sense. With the potential roadblocks removed, Mom and Dad then went after my less serious, but still present, desires.

Mom doubled down on her stance on looks. They had never mattered to her to begin with, and if I acquiesced, she could potentially still get a doctor son-in-law. She hadn't given up all hope of that yet. Dad went after what he saw as an equally debatable restriction. I had always liked taller men—personal preference. Dad, however, had always thought that too significant a height difference between the female and male looked odd. When I had mentioned that I liked men at least six feet tall, Dad said such a pairing would look mismatched since I was only five feet four inches tall. I didn't agree, and since that was in the eye of the beholder, I kept my preference initially.

But how long could that last with these two on the case? Dad would often remind me that the number of tall men, particularly from our ancestral country, was limited, and to limit the already limited pool any further could be detrimental. Seeing the potential crop, I started to see that he was right. Taller single men were definitely in the minority. So, with time, my height preference slowly fell like auction bidding in reverse. *Do I hear five foot ten inches? Going once, going twice. We have five foot eight inches. Going once, going twice. Oh, I hear five foot seven inches. Going once, going twice, sold!* I could hear the sound of gavel to wood as the word "settle" threatened my future as Mrs. Tall-dark-and-handsome.

Fortunately, or unfortunately, our people are excellent negotiators and hagglers, and do not take anything less than bargains upon bargains. So, although I was willing to sell out at five-foot-seven-inches, such a deal did not go quite far enough for Mom and Dad.

"Beta, I'm saying you shouldn't be so particular and at least come down to five-feet-six inches. That is more reasonable and will create more options."

"I'd like him to be taller than me with heels on, is all." I argued. I had already had a prom date for whom I had to bend down to hug goodnight and wear the flattest of the flats to not tower over him, and I did not want that in my husband. Pictures are for life.

"Five foot six inches is not too short. That's my height, and Mom is the same height as you," said Dad.

"Dad, you're five-seven, not five-six."

"No, look at my driver's license. It says I'm five-six."

"Dad, you're the one who tells the DMV your height, so they put whatever you say. Besides, you've probably

86

shrunk from osteoporosis." Who proudly reduces their height? Men buy shoes to make themselves taller and exaggerate all the time. But not Dad—he goes in the opposite direction!

With as many of my criteria layers as possible having been forcibly stripped, Mom and Dad turned their attention back to the serious situation at hand—a thirty-plus-year-old unmarried daughter. *Hai Ram!*

I say that as if their attention was ever elsewhere. Such a grave situation can never be anywhere but at the forefront of a parent's mind. Everywhere they went, almost every conversation they had somehow landed upon me. They grieved and lamented with friends in similar situations; picky daughters beyond marriageable age slowly quieting the hopeful sounds of the pitter-patter of little feet.

With strangers, they tried making lemonade, albeit sour, from their life lemons. Parents were crafty and solution-oriented, taking any opportunity to score a husband for their daughters; trips to the temple, office parties, doctor visits—oh yes, forget their medical ailments and check the male doctor's left ring finger; no stone would be left unturned.

They would insist I attend every event we were invited to in case a potential's parents were in attendance and happened to see me. Attending was only part of the package. I had to, of course, always dress my best, you know, just in case, and make sure I answered all questions appropriately.

Early on, I had learned that for some questions, there is only one answer. For example, when asked, typically by an aunty, if I cooked, the answer was emphatically "yes." Initially, I would answer "no." Yes, Mom and Dad had taught me how to cook. They would not have let me leave their house without knowing how to do so. Sure, they felt it important for me to be able to feed myself, but there was another motive. Everyone knows that the way to a man's heart is through food, so a girl who knows how to cook has already won half the battle. Furthermore, in traditional households, it is the wife who does the cooking, so girls need to learn how to cook to keep their new spouse and families happy.

The problem was, I never really enjoyed cooking, so I didn't do much of it. I especially didn't cook Indian food since Mom would always send me back to my apartment with a freezer full of her tasty home-cooked food. So, I would casually say I didn't cook to the aunties when asked.

When Mom heard this, she was quite upset. "Just because you don't cook much, doesn't mean you don't know how to cook. So, why do you say 'no'? It's not lying if you say 'yes'. Both are pretty much the same. Besides, what will people think? They will say, 'Her mother hasn't done her duty and taught her how to cook.' The fault and shame will always come back to the mother." Not having realized I was breaking an unwritten rule and shaming Indian mothers, including my own, I promptly corrected my erroneous ways.

Another question that needed to be answered "correctly" was age. Now, this didn't just apply to my answering of such questions, but to Ayaan and Dad's answering as well. And, in this situation, honesty was definitely not the best policy. Once, Dad was asked his and Mom's ages, and he answered accurately! *Can you believe his audacity?* Oh, was Mom livid, and she let all of us know it. For days, the pots and pans banged loudly, and the sighs of frustration overshadowed all. *How could he reveal such information?*

Dad seemed confused. What was so personal in revealing their ages? Mom was so dismayed that Dad didn't see the error of his ways, and that she had to even explain! In doing so, people would presumptively by proxy know that they had an over thirty-year-old unmarried daughter—*and who would publicly volunteer such a fact?* No one of right mind, that's who!

Mom made it clear to Ayaan as well, since he liked to post things on social media, like on birthdays. This was one of those cases where incorrect was most certainly correct—and apparently, age is not *just* a number.

A Mother's Regrets

W hen you're faced with a problem, you often step back, reflect, and try to find a solution. Well, that is after you spend copious amounts of time figuring out how said situation came to be in the first place, right? The proverbial, how and why?

Being faced with the most quizzical and worrisome situation of all, my over thirty-year-old Nikki still being unmarried, has forced me to spend a lot of time reflecting and theorizing.

How could this possibly be? Did I go wrong? If so, where and how? I must have raised too simple a daughter.

Most girls are smarter in the ways of the world. They see what they want and go after it. They don't hesitate to chase and pursue the prize. They are aggressive and bold, or as those of my generation say, *chalak*. These *chalak* girls know how to talk to guys. They also don't mind calling first, asking guys out, being persistent, and then following the men to where the men's lives take them.

Forget minding, girls do it happily, all in the pursuit of their future husband. Why isn't Nikki more like that? If she were, then she would have been long married. But how could she be? If her own mother isn't chalak, then where would she learn to be? No one in our family is that way. That's not who we are. It's just not in our family's nature. So, what can be done?

Many women have a certain "nakhra" or attitude and air about them. They don't just smile and give attention so easily. They make others come to them. They don't play hard to get; they naturally epitomize it. These same women take extra care of their appearance. They regularly get manicures, pedicures, and facials, have their hair done often, and wear makeup daily.

"Beta, you should have a bit more nakhra. You see how people flock to the girls with it? And why don't you wear any makeup? Look at these girls. Even eighteen-year-olds are routinely wearing those fake eyelashes these days. They get all dressed up and wear makeup whenever they go out. If these young girls can do it every day, why can't you?"

This is also my doing. I didn't teach her to have nakhra. Nikki couldn't have learned by observation because neither I nor anyone in our family has it. Whatever your nature is, that will remain. It's impossible to change your core ways. *She can have her nails done and get facials, though. She can wear makeup regularly, too.* That is also my fault. I never spent much time on these things myself, so she never adopted them. I didn't allow her to wear makeup in high school. I always told her that those who look good without makeup are the prettiest. Men should like you for your natural beauty and who you are. Anyway, she doesn't need much makeup to look beautiful. God has been kind. She could make a little more effort, though. I keep telling her, "You never know who sees you when you go out. Always best to be prepared."

These are only small parts of the problem. Maybe the real issue is that I was too strict and didn't allow her to date when she was in school. I didn't give her freedom. I thought that was the right way, but now look, *she's unmarried.* Her friends' mothers allowed their daughters to date starting in high school, and look, those girls are all well-settled—with children! *Meri mat hi mar gai thi. Pehlay kyon nahi socha is baath ko?* (My thinking was warped. Why didn't I think like this, *and about this*, before?)

If only I had realized and known sooner, then maybe things would have been different. But what can be done? I did the best I knew how and what I thought was right at the time, and she has turned out well. Nikki is a good girl. I just wish she had listened to me and met someone in school. I keep saying, the best time to meet someone is when you're in school, but did this girl of mine do what I said? Of course not. These kids always think they know better than us. Then later they suffer—and make us suffer with them.

Come to think of it, maybe this is all because I educated her too much. I wanted her to be a doctor. I always thought that girls should study and become financially independent. They should have a stable, rewarding career. I still believe and support that, but maybe I should have been content with her just getting a bachelor's degree.

I remember my old friend Manju telling me when our girls were young, she only wanted her daughter Rita to get a degree from a good college and stop studying after that. "Why should she study more? That's plenty. Enough to get a job and meet a boy. Then she will get married." She was right, it turned out exactly as she wanted for her daughter.

Shanti told me that boys are intimidated by highly educated women. Many boys, even doctors themselves, don't want doctor wives. Look at Sita's son, a highly trained specialist doctor who specifically wanted a non-doctor wife. That is really a shame, but on the other hand there is some sense to it. If both husband and wife are busy doctors, then who will look after the children and the home? Neither will have time for these things or each other. And in these matters, mostly it is the girl who has to sacrifice. But I cannot change the past and undo what is done.

Actually, the real problem is her focus. She has been telling me for years that she doesn't have time to search dating websites and continually meet people. What is this *"no time"* business? She thinks that focusing on medical school, residency, fellowship, and then work is an excuse?

Sure, it may have been a bit tough and required some time, but many other people do it. They know how to multitask. When I was her age, I did ten times more than she does. I had a husband to please, two small children to care for, three meals a day to cook, endless chores to complete, work during the day, and school to attend during the evening. I didn't even have any help. And yet, she can't even manage to have time to find a boy and get married.

I was never tired and she's always telling me how fatigued she is after just working during the day. Her priorities are all wrong. I'm sure of it. I'm telling her, if she can't handle working and finding a husband, then she should quit working and make this her full-time job. Anjali said the same thing to her daughter. Unless these girls completely focus on this, they will never be married. But this girl, she doesn't take me seriously. How many times am I going to tell her the same thing?

I have been too lenient. That's what her aunt told me. In fact, one of her dad's friends said the same thing. We haven't given her a deadline or any ultimatums. Some relatives have told us that if Nikki were their daughter, they would have made her marry by now. Nonsense. *How?* Shall I tie her up and drag her to the *mandap*? She is very lucky we are not those types of parents. We have never forced her into anything.

But maybe the problem is that children in America don't listen. Children in India are different. We listened to every single thing our parents said without question. In fact, we never even thought to question. Everyone did what their parents said and were happy doing so. That was the way and society was better then.

Maybe if we hadn't immigrated here from India in the first place, things would be different. I would have been a grandparent of several by now. Forget it. There's no point in thinking about any of these things. It doesn't change anything.

I was thinking, maybe…

Times,
They Are a Changin'

They say desperate times call for desperate measures. I believe the interpretation of this is purposefully left open because the meaning of desperate times can be highly variable. Most people don't like to admit that they're desperate. However, when it comes to Indian parents, particularly mothers, they have no qualms about sounding the alarms of desperation when it comes to their unmarried daughters. Nor do they experience much delay in reaching high levels of desperation in this matter.

Mom was no exception to the rule. She was desperate to get me married and had no shame in admitting it. Why should she have shame? Anyone in her shoes would clearly feel the same. And to those not in her shoes? Well, let's just say it would definitely conjure a lot of sympathy.

Mom and her friends often shared their regrets concerning their unmarried children. These discussions would occasionally spring forth ideas to rectify potential past mistakes, as many of them believed themselves to be at least partly culpable for their children's lack of success in the marriage department. They considered it their ongoing responsibility to guide (aka strong-arm) their children—(aka us adult women.)

"Hi Aunty, how are you?" I asked greeting Mom's longtime friend at a gathering.

"Hi Nikki beta, how are you? Come sit next to me. We haven't had a chance to talk in quite some time," she replied, patting the empty chair next to her. I looked around for a quick getaway, but to no avail. I had a feeling about where this little "catch-up" was headed.

"How is everything? Any good news?" Ahh, there it was. This was "Aunty code" for "Have you found anyone to marry?" My impulse was to raise my diamond ring-less left hand and say, "Does this look like 'good news' to you?" But such a snarky comeback was frowned upon when it came to the "aunty" or "uncle" communique, so I settled for a simple, "Everything's fine—and no good news."

"It's okay, beta. My Anjali has unfortunately not yet found anyone either—and she's older than you. I told her the other day though, if you need to live with a guy first to get married, that's okay, go ahead and do that. You don't need to announce it, but do it if you need to. I told your mom this too. We need to accept whatever means necessary," Aunty quietly told me. *Wait! What?* This aunty was telling me that their generation was now cool with girls living with boys?

Growing up, everything girl-boy related had been taboo and stigmatized. Girls and boys of eligible age talking alone publicly? *Bad, taboo.* Dating? *Bad, taboo.* Physical interactions—even hand holding? *Very bad, taboo.* Living with someone of the opposite sex? *Very, very bad, completely taboo.* Having a child out of wedlock? *Unfathomably bad, double taboo, and extreme condemnation.*

Yet, here we were, suddenly being told it was *alright* to live with someone of the opposite sex prior to marriage!

Yes, in recent years things had slowly changed as more of the "children" remained unmarried, but this was one gigantic leap forward for Indian man and womankind. Agreed, that over time, restrictions were loosened, and increasingly "Western ways" were adopted by most parents with each lost year of possible grandparenthood.

Initially, there was spurning of the "boys on one side and girls far away on the other" philosophy, and encouragement of girls and boys of marriageable age to talk to one another as often and widely as possible. In fact, as much as our parents could force and make it happen, they did.

Male of marriageable age spotted. Aunty beelines toward single female (daughter, relative, family friend—anyone who could benefit from her keen eye.) Said female, in the midst of conversation, is interrupted mid-sentence or mid-word, even with, "Beta, I need to speak with you, come with me," and then immediately whisked away by the arm to the possibly eligible (no time to waste on predetermining) male. "Hello. You two should talk. Go on now. Don't worry, I'm not staying," says Aunty, walking away, but only far enough to appear out of sight, but close enough to be within earshot to try and see if the conversation is going as well as planned. Of course, they never saw any awkwardness in being so "helpful."

Then, as the decade passed, it slowly became "alright" to date. Well, alright, in so much as parents weren't really given a choice in the matter. Their sons and daughters had insisted upon it and just started dating. Parents—not given much of a choice—were left to console themselves with figuring, if it was going to lead to the desired end goal of marriage, then what was the reason to protest? Besides, since essentially everyone's children were doing it at this point, it became generally "accepted."

However, it still wasn't really discussed amongst themselves. It was still somewhat stigmatized, so not

30 is a Dirty Word

considered a polite topic of conversation. So, while it was known, it was a quiet, under-the-table sort of acceptance. Most parents knew it was happening, *but why air such laundry?*

Physical interaction of any kind, however, never gained any sort of acceptance. That has always remained totally stigmatized. Indians, creators of the Kama Sutra, like their chastity. Thus, their generation preferred a don't ask, don't tell policy. It was much easier that way to ignore rumors, and hearsay, and pretend their children weren't engaging in any of the sexual activities people said kids did these days.

So, by extension, it had seemed to me that living together with the opposite sex would remain taboo as well, given the associated physical interaction implications. I mean, a one-bedroom apartment with one queen-sized bed left very little room for questioning with parents. I think they just assumed one person slept in the bedroom with the door locked, and any accidental physical touch occurring while going about the day was apologized for immediately, and then carefully avoided after that.

The whole notion of physicality had to be swept completely under the rug for parents to sleep soundly without nightmares about what people would say— because here we were upon the day when the highly taboo had become acceptable. I never gave desperation enough credit for the level of adaptation it could inspire.

Having believed to be at the limit of expansion of Indian parents' adaptation to the "Western ways," I was lulled into complacency. Therefore, I did not at all anticipate the latest bombshell to be dropped by our mothers. As their daughters remained unmarried longer and longer, our mothers' concerns grew infinitely. They

98

not only worried that we would be alone without a partner in this world if they departed (their words, clearly), but that we might miss the wondrous opportunity to have children. How would society, one in which the Indian subcontinent has over 1.4 billion people, go on otherwise?

Their fear manifested in oh-so-helpful ways. First, it was informing us, many of whom were doctors ourselves, that after thirty-five, having a child would be increasingly difficult due to a woman's finite egg supply. Not only that, but with advanced maternal age, the risk of genetic abnormalities greatly increased.

When such conversations failed to make us marry and have children immediately (forget making most of us feel bad— they were well past empathy at this stage), it became time to point out other shortcomings. "When you were young, you used to say we were old but look at yourself. You're a decade older than I was when I had you! Your children won't call you old, they'll call you ancient and resent the fact that you're too feeble to take care of them." We'd suddenly gone from eligible marriage material to wheelchair-bound geriatric nuisances overnight.

"Life is created in three phases, and things should be done in proper time. The first phase is for education and career. Children should be had by, or in the second, not third phase of life, which should be for retirement and activities such as spiritual growth," parents would say to all of us who remained single. Back to the *timing-is-everything* philosophy. Apparently, growth is not required to come with age.

Lastly, our parents tried guilt, "If you don't get married and have children soon, then we will be too old to help you. Already, we have some health problems, but we can still help raise your kids. In a few years, who knows what our health will be like and whether we will be capable of doing much for you and your children. Who knows if we will even be in this world to see your children at all." Cue the disappointed shake of the head and tear-filled eyes.

When such inspiring words shockingly only saddened rather than spurred any of us to marriage and subsequent reproduction, our parents were at a loss and disheartened. They were forced to concede that no matter what they did, there was a possibility that some of us would not get married *in time*—or heaven forbid—at all. The thought of their children without anyone to call their own was too much to bear for most of our parents. So, rumblings and suggestions of a solution started amongst themselves, and one day exploded and blew our minds.

"Beta, you know that I have two daughters. One is married and just had her first child. My other daughter is not yet married. She loves her niece like her own. But I told her, you cannot depend on that for the long term. Yes, she is like your own child, but she isn't yours. So, I told her that if she doesn't find anyone in the next two years, then she should have a baby on her own via a sperm donor. There are options these days, it's not like in our times. She asked me, 'What would people think and say?' I told her, 'Don't worry about that. It's important for you to have someone of your own for your future.'"

I was beyond dumbfounded listening to this aunty speak to me at another gathering. This couldn't be popular thinking amongst the parents. The fact that this aunty was less concerned about what people would think clearly indicated how progressive she was. Maybe she was a lone bird in this line of thought. That could be the only reasonable explanation. That, or that aliens had taken over her brain. Both options were equally plausible in this case.

Apparently, aliens *had* come to earth and overtaken the brains of many Indian parents, including Mom's. "Beta, it is very important for you to have someone. We do not want you to be alone. You have seen, when people get married, they get busy. Their priorities naturally shift to their new families. You have seen that no one really has time for anyone else. Even siblings. We will always be here for you, but we will not live forever. Then what? Having your own child through science before time runs out will at least give you someone of your own. If it's the only option, then it's better than nothing. Sheila and Anjali both told me that they each told their daughters the same thing. We are all ready to support you." *Mind completely blown!*

What had happened to extreme condemnation for having a child out of wedlock and thus being the source of dishonor and shame beyond belief to parents, extended family, onlookers, the community as a whole, and all of society in general? Where had being the resultant subject of shock, horror, disapproval, reproach, and gossip for all of time, gone? Far more importantly, how could we possibly live with what people would think and say?

The only saving grace was that the loophole of science allowed for the preservation of chastity and no sex before marriage. Thank the lord, or shall we say science, which surprisingly in this situation, was working hand in hand with the church—and they say oil and water don't mix. Add to it the aliens that had taken over the brains of Indian parents, and we had the unimaginable trifecta.

Times, they really were changing, and unbelievably and ironically, the forward movement was driven by generally backward-thinking Indian parents.

Quick, look outside, do you see the pigs flying?

Jump Ship
Before You Too Drown

Having a sibling is one of life's greatest gifts. They are your first friend, playmate throughout childhood, commiseration partner, and teammate to stand a chance against your parents. Siblings are the only ones who truly understand the impact of developmental familial experiences on personalities and life choices. They may bother you, get you into trouble, and fight with you—ad nauseam, but they love and support you always. I was lucky to have such a sibling. Yes, we fought endlessly, but we could always count on one another to have each other's backs in anything. All those projects I did and papers I wrote for him throughout school had to count for something after all.

When it came to the crusade on my single life waged by Mom and Dad, I had Ayaan to count on to make the fight at least a little more even. When they pressured me, he calmly and impartially talked with them to explain my point of view and convince them to ease off. When Mom and Dad made what I considered unreasonable requests, Ayaan served as the go-between, finding a middle ground that appeased us all. When I was exasperated with situations, he provided advice and suggestions on how to see things differently. When Mom and Dad were too invasive and wouldn't let up with their interrogation concerning my future, Ayaan came to my defense, redirecting and then ending their barrage of questions. He was always on my side—until one day—he wasn't.

My parents' patience with me as the offspring frontrunner for marriage was running on empty. Dates, matchmakings, fixer-uppers, and hopeful encounters had all failed to deliver a son-in-law, so they set their sights on the next best thing—a daughter-in-law. Ayaan's career as an amused spectator and sideline coach was coming to an end. I watched in amusement as my parents' attention began to shift from me to the next possible solution to their quest to become doting grandparents, Ayaan.

"I was talking to Rita aunty, and she was telling me that she told her children that someone should get things started and get married already. It's true. Doesn't matter who starts, but someone please get married. What is going on with you these days?" Mom asked, turning to Ayaan, who was quietly sitting at the table, eating lunch. It was as if marriage were a bandwagon, and if one person jumped on, it would automatically make all the other single children do so as well. It appeared as though this bandwagon, coughing along with deflated tires and an empty tank, needed the jumpstart of one sacrificial single child to breathe new life into it. They do say peer pressure is very real and consequential.

"We continually have parents suggesting their daughters for you," said Mom. "So many nice girls are recommended for you. Have you been in contact with any of them? What happened with Seema's daughter? She was the one whose picture we most recently showed you. Seema tells me she is a very nice girl. I hear she is very smart and respectful."

"I didn't think she was good-looking. She wasn't for me," replied Ayaan, barely looking up from his meal. I was suddenly jealous of his ability to shut her down so nonchalantly. Whatever her response, he anticipated it and had a comeback. It was akin to watching Agassi, one of tennis' greatest returners, at work. Over the years, he had watched, listened, planned, and pocketed all the defense mechanisms I was too polite to use in force, and now played them expertly. I had unknowingly trained my brother to be the quintessential bachelor who didn't give a damn and wasn't about to have his life plan thrust under his nose.

"What do you mean not good-looking? You have these ridiculous standards. Rejecting such a nice girl for no reason! What about Reena's niece? She is a very pretty girl, and a doctor too. Have you called and met with her yet?" One had to admire her tenacity, even on this journey to certain defeat.

"Nope, not interested," was all Ayaan replied. I was dumbfounded. How did he think he would get away without providing any more details than that? He was clearly misguided and uninformed in this department. The investigative department that was our parents could hardly be satisfied with such little intel. They needed to know the time, date, exact words, and detailed outcome of every interaction. If it wasn't provided to their satisfaction, how else could they, along with the potential match's parents, communicate and be overly involved?

"What is this 'not interested' business? How could you possibly find something wrong with such a nice girl? Tell me, why don't you like her? You know, you're almost thirty yourself. If you keep rejecting all these girls this way, you're not going to find anyone. You'll be single just like Nikki."

"Speaking of Nikki, aren't you guys worried? Don't you think you should be focusing on her? You really should be. She's well past thirty and still hasn't found anyone. The pool of potential guys is even smaller now.

Aren't you concerned?" Ayaan asked with a serious tone. Mom suddenly turned towards me and eyed me with despair.

"This girl, she doesn't listen! Over thirty and still won't compromise. It's Saturday, and she's here sitting at home again! Why do you stay home with us so much? Shouldn't you be out on a date? Or maybe at an event where you could meet someone? How will you get married like this? Hai Ram," Mom exclaimed in exasperation.

Meanwhile, like a baby pig bathed in olive oil, Ayaan slipped out of the kitchen. Oh, this was rich. I saw exactly what he was doing. This throwing of the "she's not married" grenade to cause a distraction from himself, leading to an explosion that only wounded me, was the work of a diabolical genius, also known as Ayaan. Too bad Mom didn't see this blatant bait-and-switch scheme, and fell for it each time he did it, which was fairly often.

I tried flipping the script and turning his own tactic on him. Unfortunately, Mom always thwarted my efforts, and of course, the conversation would fall back onto my unmarried-ness. When Mom would ask me if I had been on any dates recently, I would ask her to take a break from focusing on me and think about Ayaan, who was also single and getting older. He, too, deserved her attention after all.

"We get so many suggestions for girls for Ayaan. We look and ask for you but instead come back with several biodatas of girls for him. If he showed any interest or said the word, there would be so many potential girls for him. But Ayaan doesn't even look at our suggestions. He doesn't listen, so we've just left it to him. He'll find someone, we know it. We're not really worried about him.

You, on the other hand, we are very worried about, as you have yet to find anyone or be serious. What are we going to do with you? Why don't you reconsider that one boy that Tina said she knows in Seattle? So, he doesn't want to move. You'll get used to all that rain, it's tropical, like Bali." I wanted to laugh until I realized she was totally serious.

Somehow, the plan that worked so well for Ayaan not only failed miserably for me but actually made the conversation worse at times. He found it funny that I was always the only casualty in his maniacal plan. I had to admit, while I rightfully hated his traitorous behavior, it was wildly successful. He escaped unfettered for years. A few moments of questioning and frustration from Mom and Dad were the most he ever received, even after he, too, turned thirty!

He had a knack for avoiding conversations on his return from a date. Like some kind of Houdini, he'd disappear only to reappear when enough time had passed that Mom and Dad were onto something else—usually my dates, or lack thereof. I could go on about the unfairness of the situation and the unequal treatment of the two of us, but let's be honest, nothing is fair in life. And while parents love all their children equally, the scrutiny can be far from even. To Ayaan, all the extra attention I received was because I was their favorite. *Lucky me!*

The interesting thing about this scheme of Ayaan's was the shift that occurred somewhere along the course. Initially, the waving of the wand in his right hand to distract from the cookie in his left hand was to save himself from the marriage conversations with Mom and Dad. But just like a magician, what met the eye initially didn't turn out to be reality.

"Dude, this isn't fair. They don't grill you about every detail of a date. They don't lecture you that your future is bound to be lonely, full of leftovers and TV serials," I'd often complain.

"I agree, you do get a lot of pressure from Mom and Dad. I've talked to them repeatedly about backing off. You already put a lot of pressure on yourself, and their habit of piling more on isn't helpful. I've told them it'll only stress you out further and could contribute to you not making the best choice. They listen and agree, but you know they can't totally stop. They're way too worried, and honestly, to some degree, legitimately so," he hesitated before leveling a blow I didn't see coming, "Look, I don't want to be harsh, but the reality is that you're thirty-five years old now. The potential pool of available guys is small, and honestly, only getting smaller." His words stung, and I was instantly taken aback at the lack of sibling loyalty. *Weren't we a team?* United in our common lack of life partners ourselves? Didn't we *both* understand and rebel against the myopic pressure our parents placed on marriage?

"You limited it with your preferences for years, and now, unfortunately, even though you've opened up, there aren't that many options to even choose from. So, it's either you give up even more of your preferences and choose from the few available options to have a family like you want, or keep holding out for that unicorn that you're looking for and accept that it may take years and you may not have the kids or family exactly as you desire. Honestly, I'm not trying to add any pressure at all, but I'm kind of with them on you getting serious and the gravity of the situation." I was stunned. When had it gone from a smoke-and-mirrors act to reality? Who was this deserter?

Jumping ship to join the parentals, leaving me alone, aimlessly adrift? I was stunned at the obvious betrayal.

"I thought you were on my side. I thought you understood. You know what it's been like for me. Also, you yourself are over thirty and still single."

"I do, and like I said, I'm not pressuring you or trying to stress you out. I just think you might want to reevaluate the whole situation," said Ayaan, effectively ending the conversation. Honestly, I was at such a loss for words.

Ayaan didn't just talk the talk; he walked the walk, specifically off the plank of the proverbial ship. One day, a few months before his thirty-fifth birthday, he sat Mom, Dad, and me down and told us he wanted to get engaged and married to his best friend. The engagement happened a few weeks after his announcement, and the wedding later that year. Ayaan didn't waste time. Like father, like son, apparently.

Now, while this was amazing for him and our family, it brought with it many unwanted side effects for me. Being completely single, without any prospects in sight, there were some serious adverse events to be endured. You would think that his engagement and subsequent marriage would be all about him, but you'd be wrong.

Each congratulatory sentiment for Ayaan was accompanied by an equally sympathetic one for me. The awkward dance to balance the juxtaposition of joy and sorrow was exhausting for my parents.

While some relatives and family friends were more subtle, giving side glances and looks of "it's a shame," others were more direct. "Oh, still nothing has happened for your daughter. It will be even harder with your son getting married. People will wonder. Why is she being unnecessarily picky? Maybe if you quickly arrange something, she and your son can get married on the same day. There's still some time."

The remarks were relentless, "You must be thrilled for your son, but at the same time very upset that your daughter is still unmarried. She is older than him, right?" I had to constantly quell my urge to climb a mountain and shout from the very top, "Mind your own business!!!" But I knew that was an exercise in futility.

Even my parents' lobs at my impending spinsterhood were without mercy: "Beta, look, even your brother is getting married now. What are you waiting for, to be the only single person left?" and "When are you going to give us good news like your brother? We've waited too long already. You should already have adolescent children by this point."

Lucky for me, dealing with such looks and comments came with lots of unsolicited advice from other friends and family:

"So, what if it's true? Don't let it bother you."

"Take it in one ear and out the other."

"Don't feel bad, they mean well."

"Let it go. They are family who just want the best for you."

"Tell them they'll be the first to know when something happens."

"Find someone very quickly, decide, and get engaged at least. That will surely quiet everyone down."

The most common was of course, "ignore them." Easy for all of them to say since it wasn't them in the position of being the single over thirty-five-year-old sister trying to smile and push past all the chatter. I guess it was a good thing that advice flowed freely. It would come in handy over the next couple of years when my brother and his wife announced they were expecting their first child, had their son, and then soon thereafter announced and subsequently had their second child.

"They are having a child, and you still haven't even met anyone yet?"

"They had their baby, and you're still looking? You should have already had all of your children by now. That is, if God even allows you to at this point in time."

"They are having their second child, and still nothing has changed for you. This is really a shame. Are you even interested in getting married? Are you even trying?"

"They have now had their second baby, and still, you're in the same position. *Hai hai.* You're older than them, but they've moved much faster than you. You should learn a thing or two from them and follow suit as quickly as possible. There's no time left now."

It was quite rough at times, singlehandedly maneuvering this ship over the choppy, turbulent waters of the vast and extensive Indian ocean of singledom. Being the captain in such challenging situations demanded a high level of strength and patience. I will say though, meeting such demands evoked a unique sense of pride and accomplishment. Sailing my ship in my chosen direction across continents and experiencing the journey with all its breathtaking views and memorable moments was actually enjoyable, liberating, and often fulfilling.

Mom and Dad, of course, saw it differently. If you asked them, my ship appeared to be going down on what seemed like a never-ending journey to nowhere. Ayaan had managed to save himself from drowning. *Could I?* It was uncertain and only appeared to be left to the gods at this point. Good thing Mom had increased her daily prayers from one hour to two hours. That was the bare minimum required if there was any chance God would heed her prayers and save my soul from life as a spinster. The only saving grace in this situation was that my ship was going down over water, and that should hopefully put out the fires of hell that are apparently those of being an unmarried Indian girl approaching forty.

According to Mom and Dad, the world had ended at the dirtiness of thirty. Forty, now that was the most terrible, unimaginable corner of parents' minds that couldn't really exist, and therefore possibly come to fruition for their unmarried daughters. No amount of consolation could aid in the recovery from such a tragedy. At least not in this mortal world. Only if God himself proclaimed it barely acceptable could our parents' hearts and minds attempt to grasp such a mortifying, reality-defying, unthinkable absurdity. They would try, although it would be extremely difficult. Success was definitely not guaranteed.

That they would even survive through such times was uncertain, according to them. Gods, please save us all. Oh, and don't let anyone see us girls enjoying being captains of our ship and even relishing the ride. *What would people think, or worse—say?*

For Whom the Wedding Bells Toll

A journey often requires patience, and at times, a lot of it, but in the end, hard work does pay off. Prayers get answered. *Shraddha aur saburi*, or "faith and patience," as one Indian saying goes. *Bhagwan ke ghar dher hai, per andher nahi*, or "there is delay, but not darkness at God's doorstep," another popular Hindu saying promises.

This is all what *they* say, right? And thus far, *they* have been right. Right?

So apropos, it should be time for the fairytale happy ending where I tell you about a crazy, whirlwind romance that began with an online swipe right on the infamous Indian matrimonial site, just as I was on the verge of quitting the whole online dating thing. A tale of a magical connection with a tall, handsome, brilliant, witty man who just happened to be a doctor. I'd tell you how amazing our first date was, how he actually looked like his attractive photo, and how he was thoughtful, interesting, and oh-so-charming. I'd tell you how our first date turned into many and that the two of us clicked on multiple levels until he finally proposed—and I said, "Yes!" and we're getting *married* early next year!

But that's not happened.

The charming, brilliant, handsome man from the depths of my imagination has yet to get the memo to show up and forge an everlasting connection with me while expertly gaining the love and acceptance of my parents and proving to be the answer to their prayers and even sweeping Ayaan into a fun bromance.

He's still out there, somewhere in the ether, no doubt waiting to slip the glass slipper on my foot. He just seems to be cruising along on a turtle, not riding on a white horse.

And that's okay. *They* do say the journey is more important than the destination. And I've certainly been enjoying my annual trips around the sun—traveling the globe experiencing different cultures and seeing the wonders of the world, building a rewarding career caring for people as a doctor, and creating a lifetime of sweet memories in all those fun moments, small and big, with my close and cherished friends and family (yes, Ayaan too, who is still my best friend). The past twenty years of talk from others about finding someone to define me as a woman and wife has been just that, talk. I've defined myself, and it's been a pretty good, complete track for just shy of four decades on the planet if I do say so myself.

While my parents have certainly tried to bend the will of the universe and make it succumb to their own, somehow, even with all their enthusiasm, might, and even guilt, they have yet to succeed. Surprising, even to me. I didn't think anyone, including God, him or herself, could escape the powers that are the guilt-ridden tirades of an Indian mother.

Alas, Mom and Dad are not quitters and refuse to concede defeat. According to them, they will not have completed their jobs as parents or be free until I am married. Only then will they be able to bathe in the Ganges River. As if it is something they truly want to do, or that I or Ayaan would even have them do.

Don't mistake my acceptance of the current non-wedding-in-my-future climate as laying down my true love sword. I've got all the feelers on high alert for when he does stumble into my path or profile.

We really do need more feel-good stories these days, and I plan to be one of them. Wait, scratch *plan* from the last sentence. You know what happens when I or my parents plan. And God has laughed plenty already. Mom and Dad have provided so much material, I'm sure that His or Her sides hurt from being doubled over. I think it's about time that we got in on the laughter. *They* do say it's the best medicine after all, and I appreciate a good dose. Trust me—I'm a doctor. You already know to trust *them*.

While laughter may be touted as a good treatment, it's certainly no cure, according to Mom and Dad. Since there hasn't been any laughter in this vortex, they're going to need to see the studies of its effectiveness before adopting such a foreign concept. This isn't a laughing matter in their playbook after all. It's the final minute of the Super Bowl, and a "Hail Mary" seems to be their only option. Definitely avoid overtime at all costs. To them, time's a-wastin'.

I have no crystal ball to tell you what happens next. Will my parents finally see their daughter to wedded bliss? Maybe. Hopefully, if for no other reason than to finally stop hearing about how I should have considered and married Raj. Gone are the days when marriage and babies into your 40s were unheard of. In fact, people who marry later enjoy close, stable relationships because they know what they want, they're likely financially stable and seek higher levels of companionship, happily skipping the drama and pain of a marriage of desperation in their 20s. *God, can you please send this memo to Mom and Dad ASAP?* You know they likely will listen to no one else.

So, your reward for witnessing my journey on these pages so far will have to wait. But not to worry, I'm quite content with the present company of me-myself-and-I for the time being, and I plan to keep choosing wisely.

Hemingway said it best, "No man (or woman) is an island"—at least not forever. In the meantime, there are bound to be some pretty amazing sunsets.

I'll take them.

Raising my tropical drink to you—till we meet again.

The End (for now)

About the Author

Nishi Gulati is an avid world traveler, a health and fitness enthusiast, and a huge fan of dark chocolate. She loves seeing and experiencing cultures, historical sites, and natural wonders, mostly by walking, and is often planning her next adventure abroad. She is a physician by profession, and a commentator of life by heart.

She believes the best art imitates life—hence this book where she opens up about the secret "funny cause its true" world and ironic experiences of first-generation Indian adults in the "most important" part of their lives. Join her on this journey and trust her—she's a doctor.

.